Strategic Indicators for Higher Education, 1996

by

Barbara E. Taylor
and
William F. Massy

Peterson's
Princeton, New Jersey

Acknowledgments

Above all, we are indebted to the nearly 1,000 colleges and universities that provided the data presented and analyzed in this book. In an era of downsizing, we know that information requests from external researchers can present an added burden to already overtaxed staff. We are grateful that so many saw our work as important enough to warrant their time and attention, and we hope the results justify their efforts.

The staff at Peterson's Guides administered the survey, entered the data, and created the initial database with their usual competence and professionalism. Kimberly Hoeritz was our principal contact at Peterson's and worked with us ably from survey development through publication. Ted Bross of Thomas Jefferson University developed and managed with great skill the database used for statistical analysis, and he responded cheerfully to numerous requests for additional analyses. We also adapted, with permission from our friend and colleague Joel W. Meyerson, some material he wrote for the first edition of Strategic Indicators for Higher Education. We thank him for his generosity.

Barbara E. Taylor
Washington, D.C.

William F. Massy
Stanford, California

Table of Contents

Fund-Raising

Students—Tuition, Fees, and Financial Aid

Faculty

Introduction

In 1993, Peterson's, in cooperation with the Association of Governing Boards of Universities and Colleges (AGB), published the first edition of *Strategic Indicators for Higher Education.* This second edition of Strategic Indicators expands on the first by analyzing a larger and broader database of information about the condition of colleges and universities across the United States.

Higher education continues to face one of the most challenging environments in its history. As we wrote in 1993, colleges and universities are under intense pressure to restructure and reform. Critics, including many who believe the American system of higher education is the best in the world, believe that the enterprise is inefficient and wasteful. The national economy in which colleges and universities operate is under severe stress, and colleges and universities, including even the best managed and most wealthy, feel themselves to be under severe financial distress. As a result, many are being forced to scale back programs and personnel. Costs are rising, and many families are finding it difficult to afford college, especially as increasing numbers of traditional college-aged students are found among disadvantaged groups.

In response to these challenges, many governing boards and senior managers are working together to help colleges and universities curb random growth, rein in spiralling costs, and stem institutional drift. Indeed, they are helping to create strategically focused institutions committed to achieving distinctive competence in core programs today and to attaining essential institutional goals in the future. To accomplish this, boards and managers together are thinking strategically—defining a vision, setting institutional priorities, balancing current and future needs, and monitoring institutional performance.

Strategic thinking requires objectivity, an honest assessment of how an institution is doing and where it is heading—that is, its strategic position. This is where *Strategic Indicators for Higher Education* comes in. The second edition of *Strategic Indicators,* along with its predecessor, are the outgrowth of two pioneering studies published by the Association of Governing Boards of Universities and Colleges—*Strategic Analysis: Using Comparative Data to Understand Your Institution* and *Strategic Decision Making: Key Questions and Indicators for Trustees.* All four books are based on the use of indicators, which are ratios, percentages, or other quantitative values that allow an institution to compare its position in key strategic areas to competitors, to past performance, or to goals set previously. In commerce and economics, common indicators include the unemployment rate, the Consumer Price Index, and measures of housing starts. In higher education, one is apt to hear about indicators such as the student-faculty ratio, yield on endowment, and percentage of applicants accepted for admission. In either case, the use is the same. Indicators enable decision makers to assess an institution's strategic position through comparative analysis.

Many institutions find it extremely difficult to conduct this kind of analysis because they lack timely, reliable information on key strategic values from comparable institutions. *Strategic Indicators* responds to this need by analyzing more than 100 key indicators based on data collected from nearly 1,000 institutions.

In selecting indicators, we were governed by the following tenet: Since trustees and other institutional leaders do not have the time to analyze all (or even most) available information, they must focus on areas most likely to affect the success of their institution, that is, those areas most likely to influence its performance and strategic position over the long term. These critical success factors will not be the same for all institutions but will vary depending on size, control, location, history, mission, goals, and other factors. For example, a non-selective, tuition-dependent private college will avidly monitor applications, acceptances, and "yield" (the percentage of accepted applicants who matriculate). A research university will watch trends in receipt of federal research dollars. A public community college that wants to increase the proportion of graduates that transfer to four-year institutions will monitor that indicator.

Included among the indicators this book are most of the measures most institutions should monitor, but this is not an exhaustive list. The diversity of the higher education enterprise is such that no single listing of indicators could reflect comprehensively the condition of all institutions with their varying circumstances, missions, and strategies. For example, a church-related college may wish to watch the percentage of total revenues provided by the sponsoring denomination, an indicator not provided in this book. Readers should begin with the indicators provided here and then ask themselves, "What else do we need to know in order to understand the condition of our institution?"

HOW TO USE STRATEGIC INDICATORS

Strategic Assets. A powerful method of analyzing strategic performance is to perceive an institution as comprising four fundamental strategic assets. These are:

- Financial capital
- Physical capital
- Information capital
- Human capital

Financial capital is an institution's economic resources—its revenue and reserves, investments, and endowment. Physical capital consists of buildings, land, and equipment. Information capital is library and computer resources. And Human capital is the intellectual wealth of an institution—its students, faculty, and staff. The quality of these assets—and their interrelationships—drives an institution's strategic condition.

Strategic Indicators. For each type of strategic asset, we have selected a number of key strategic indicators that capture the meaning and value of that area. Some indicators are more accurate measures than others. For instance, financial indicators such as endowment yield and tuition and fee income per student are precise and reliable. Others are less so but serve as good proxies for the desired information. For example, we have used as an indicator of deferred maintenance the ratio of the estimated maintenance backlog to the total replacement value of plant. Both the maintenance backlog and the replacement value of plant are inexact measures, but we believe the ratio is the best easily calculated indicator of the condition of the physical plant. Generally, we chose indicators that are well understood, widely accepted, and easy to compute using data readily available to most institutions.

Comparisons. To assess strategic performance and position, it is often necessary to compare a college or university with similar institutions. We collected an analyzed data for six separate "peer" groups—three each for public and private institutions.

- *Public*

  Two-year colleges

  Regional colleges and universities

  Research universities

• *Private*

Tuition and fees less than $9,000

Tuition and fees between $9,000 and $12,000

Tuition and fees more than $12,000

These groupings have allowed apt comparisons in recent studies, and most are self-explanatory. However, two require clarification. Public regional colleges and universities include institutions eligible for membership in the American Association of State Colleges and Universities (AASCU). Public research universities include institutions eligible for membership in the National Association of State Universities and Land Grant Colleges (NASULGC) or the Association of American Universities (AAU). (Institutions eligible for membership in both AASCU and NASULGC have been included in the second category.)

Analysis. Each strategic indicator is accompanied by a narrative and visual analysis. The narrative analysis 1) details the significance of each indicator, 2) interprets the findings for each peer group, and 3) poses questions trustees and other decision makers might ask about that area. The visual analysis arrays for each peer group the average indicator value along with percentile distributions.

In most cases, we report median values. The median represents the midpoint value in a distribution, with an equal number of values above and below it. The median often is a more useful measure of central tendency than the mean, which can be misleading if a distribution contains a few very low or very high values. Percentiles are presented for the 5th, 50th, and 95th percentiles. The 50th percentile is the median, and the 5th and 95th percentiles are estimates of the realistic range of values in the distribution, absent extreme outliers. Pie charts and numerical tables, where included, are based on mean values, rather than medians, so that items in the charts or tables will sum to approximately 100 percent.

Before Beginning . . . some advice and caveats are in order.

• In starting out, a board and administration may want to analyze as many applicable indicators as possible in order to identify current or potential problem areas for the institution. Subsequently, institutional leaders can develop a shorter list of measures that must be monitored continuously or periodically, either because they suggest the institution is at risk in some way or because they are deemed essential to the achievement of the institution's strategy.

• It is important to note that there is no "right" or "wrong" value for any indicator. What is essential is to know an institution's position relative to peers, to past performance, or to goals, and to understand the reasons for any disparities noted.

• The data presented here are national norms for broadly defined peer groups. An institution may want to collect and analyze comparative data for other kinds of peer groups, such as the institutions with which it competes for students, fellow colleges and universities in a state system, or those that are affiliated with a common religious denomination.

• In addition to analyzing comparative institutional data, it is important to bear in mind the external trends and influences not directly reflected in the indicators presented here. For example, public universities must monitor political and economic trends in the state that will affect appropriations. Community colleges must monitor local business trends for clues about needed new programs. Religiously affiliated colleges must study trends in church membership and denominational support for higher education.

Caveats notwithstanding, *Strategic Indicators* provides a framework for understanding institutional condition and taking steps to improve competitive position. Readers will find the following information in the pages that follow:

1. We begin by describing the Top Ten indicators, those that many institutions will want to assess first and monitor regularly.

2. The body of the book presents more than 100 indicators, including the Top 10, and provides a description of each indicator, an analysis of the peer group data, a short list of questions trustees and top administrators might ask to understand their institution's condition with respect to that indicator, and a graphic display of the data.

3. At the end of the book are notes on survey methodology and response rates, the survey instrument, a glossary of terms used in the survey and the book, and the formulas used to calculate the indicators.

Top Ten Indicators

Some indicators may be more revealing than others for a particular institution. For example, a research university will want to monitor trends in receipt of U.S. government research funds, while a college desiring to increase the diversity of its student body will wish to track enrollments by race and ethnicity. Still, for most institutions, a handful of indicators will be especially revealing, and hence especially important to monitor. Despite vast differences among institutions, the ten indicators that follow will form the core of many institutions' "top ten" list.

1. Revenue Structure. All institutions need to understand where their revenues come from, note how stable and reliable those sources have been over time, and estimate how they may change in the future. (See page 2.)

2. Expenditure Structure. Institutions must know where they are spending their resources, what their expenditure trends are, and what these trends suggest about future financial stability. (See page 22).

3. Excess (Deficit) of Current Fund Revenues Over Current Fund Expenditures. For private colleges and universities, this measure of financial flexibility approximates the amount of time that an institution could operate without any additional infusion of funds. Most public universities are not allowed to accumulate fund balances, so this measure will not be meaningful for them. They may wish instead to monitor trends in public appropriations, per capita spending for public higher education, or the proportion of state revenues going to public higher education. (See page 30.)

4. Percent of Freshman Applicants Accepted and Percent of Accepted Freshmen Who Matriculate. While treated as separate measures in this book, these indicators are highly interrelated. The first is a measure of institutional selectivity that is crucial for all but open admissions colleges. An institution that accepts a large or growing proportion of applicants may have less control over student quality and eventually the overall size of the student body. The second indicator, a measure of admissions "yield," is an important measure of an institution's attractiveness which, with selectivity, suggests how much flexibility it has to control the quality and composition of its own student body. (See pages 121 and 124.)

5. Ratio of Full-Time-Equivalent Students to Full-Time- Equivalent Faculty. While an institution's overall ratio of students to faculty may mask significant variability among programs and departments, this measure is the starting point for assessing faculty workload and productivity. (See page 164.)

6. Institutional Scholarship and Fellowship Expenditures as a Percent of Total Tuition and Fee Income. This measure of net tuition income reflects the extent to which the institution, in effect, returns a percentage of tuition income in the form of grant aid. Both of these indicators are especially important for the private sector but are of increasing significance for public institutions as their tuitions rise. (See page 132.)

7. Tenure Status of Full-Time-Equivalent Faculty. This measure suggests how much flexibility the institution has to add faculty in areas of growing student demand or to decrease the size of the faculty if enrollments or revenues decline. (See page 147.)

8. Percent of Total Full-Time-Equivalent Employees Who Are Faculty. This indicator reflects an institution's mission and program mix, as well as its choices about the division of labor between faculty and staff. A large or growing proportion of faculty may indicate an appropriate emphasis on academic mission, or it might suggest that the institution is giving insufficient attention to administrative and support functions. (See page 171.)

9. Estimated Maintenance Backlog as a Percentage of Total Replacement Value of Plant. Deferred maintenance is a growing concern for most institutions, whose capital assets are deteriorating as scarce funds are diverted to academic and other priorities that may seem more pressing. (See page 81.)

10. Percent of Living Alumni Who Have Given at Any Time During the Past Five Years. Alumni giving is a significant source of institutional support and an important proxy for constituent opinion about institutional performance. The measure has always been important for private colleges and universities. As public institutions become more dependent on private giving, it is becoming increasingly significant for them as well. (See page 72.)

Financial Capital

Overall revenue structure

SIGNIFICANCE

An institution's overall revenue structure reflects its diversity of funding sources. It is generally believed that an institution that derives its revenues from several independent sources enjoys greater flexibility and stability. By contrast, heavy reliance on one or a very few sources—such as tuition or government appropriations—may result in greater volatility and unpredictability. At the same time, dependence on one or two sources of revenue is not necessarily dangerous, assuming those sources are dependable. For example, a tuition dependent institution that rejects a large proportion of applicants is less vulnerable than another tuition dependent college that accepts virtually all who apply. To the extent that an institution depends heavily on a single revenue source that is not absolutely reliable, it may be well advised to seek increased income diversity by developing new or enhanced sources of revenue.

INTERPRETATION

Most public institutions have more diversified revenue structures than private colleges and universities. In addition to state appropriations, public institutions receive substantial income from tuition and fees and from federal grants and contracts. Public funding—whether from appropriations or from grants and contracts—can be volatile, however, particularly during times of economic duress and regional recessions. Significantly, it is the failure of public funds to grow commensurate with need that explains significant increases in recent years in the tuition and fees public institutions charge.

For private institutions, tuition and fees are the most prominent source of revenue, representing, on average, well over half of total income. As for most public institutions, income from auxiliary enterprises also is a significant income source, but because, at least theoretically, auxiliary income is offset by its concomitant expenses, it does not contribute to overall financial strength or flexibility.

REVENUE STRUCTURE

Source	Public Two-year	Public Regional Colleges and Universities	Public Research and Land-Grant Universities	Private tuition under $9,000	Private tuition $9,000–$12,000	Private tuition over $12,000
Tuition & fees	21.6%	26.1%	20.3%	55.5%	62.6%	60.8%
Federal appropriations	0.7%	0.0%	1.2%	0.5%	0.2%	0.1%
State appropriationss	37.7%	42.3%	35.9%	0.3%	0.5%	0.5%
Local appropriationss	14.1%	0.2%	0.1%	0.0%	0.0%	0.0%
Federal grants and contracts	12.9%	9.3%	12.9%	8.5%	5.5%	4.3%
State grants and contracts	3.8%	2.9%	2.3%	3.1%	3.2%	1.4%
Local grants and contracts	0.6%	0.4%	0.4%	0.1%	0.0%	0.1%
Private gifts, grants, and contracts	0.9%	1.9%	3.5%	12.1%	7.0%	6.3%
Endowment support	0.1%	0.3%	0.4%	4.5%	3.3%	6.0%
Sales and services of educational activities	0.5%	1.5%	3.4%	0.6%	0.9%	1.0%
Sales and services of auxiliary enterprises	6.6%	13.1%	11.4%	13.6%	14.7%	16.1%
Sales and services of hospitals	0.0%	0.0%	7.2%	0.0%	0.4%	1.1%
Independent operations	0.2%	0.1%	1.0%	0.7%	0.3%	1.1%
Other revenues	.3%	1.9%		.5%	1.4%	1.2%

A note about this table: Numbers used in this table are means (the numerical average), in contrast to medians (the middle value in a distribution), which are used elsewhere in this book. In a perfectly normal distribution, the median and mean are the same. Where a distribution is highly skewed, the two values may be very different. Hence, the reader will note differences between the values in this table and those found on succeeding pages, where medians of some of the same variables are displayed and described.

QUESTIONS FOR POLICY MAKERS TO ASK

1. What are our most significant sources of revenue, and how do they compare with our peer institutions?

2. How dependent are we on one or two single revenue sources, and has this dependence increased or decreased over time?

3. What revenue sources are likely to increase or decrease over the next few years? How are we preparing for these changes?

4. Can we identify any new or enhanced sources of revenue? What are our plans for developing these sources?

Tuition and fees as a percent of total current fund revenues

SIGNIFICANCE

Tuition and fees are the primary source of revenue for private institutions and an increasingly significant source of income for public institutions as well. Across both sectors, student charges have risen faster than either wages or the rate of inflation (though increases, especially within the private sector, have begun to moderate in recent years). This rise in charges has produced both a crisis of affordability and the perception in some quarters that higher education is greedy and wasteful.

Colleges and universities respond that charges have risen for a variety of legitimate reasons. Institutions have experienced cutbacks in government support for higher education, productivity improvements that would keep cost of attendance down are much more difficult to achieve in a labor-intensive industry, and demands for new technology, physical plant improvements, and other high-ticket items are increasing rapidly. For many institutions, student financial aid is the most rapidly growing portion of the budget. As institutional costs and charges have risen, colleges and universities have been forced to allocate more of their own money—or shift costs from one student to another—to subsidize attendance by those who cannot afford to pay.

INTERPRETATION

Virtually all private institutions are tuition driven, with tuition and fees representing, on average, about 60 percent of total revenue. For public colleges and universities, tuition and fee income is also significant, second in magnitude only to state appropriations. Tuition and fees constitute about one-fifth of revenues for two-year colleges and research universities, and more than one quarter of all income for regional institutions.

TUITION AND FEES AS A PERCENT OF TOTAL CURRENT FUND REVENUES

PUBLIC

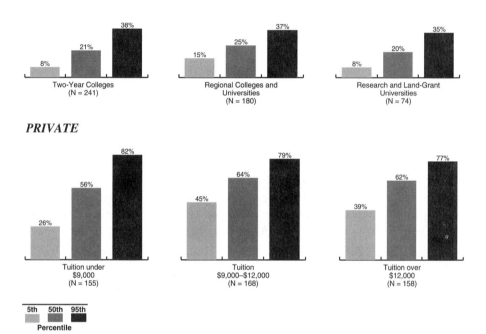

PRIVATE

QUESTIONS FOR POLICY MAKERS TO ASK

1. What percentage of our total net revenue is attributable to tuition and fee income, and how does this compare with our peer institutions?

2. Has our dependence on tuition and fee income increased or decreased over time? How stable are our other sources of income?

3. How are tuition and fee increases influencing the size, quality, and character of our student applicant pool? Our matriculation and retention rates?

4. Is our enrollment stable, and is our student mix desirable? Are any changes attributable to increases in tuition and fee charges?

State appropriations as a percent of total current fund revenues
Local appropriations as a percent of total current fund revenues

SIGNIFICANCE

State appropriations are the primary source of funding for public institutions. In addition, public two-year colleges receive significant income from local appropriations. In recent years, appropriations in most states and localities have declined or grown very slowly. The lifting of the most recent recession has improved the financial condition of most states and localities, but financial stresses and demands have grown precipitously. Government at all levels is under pressure to lower taxes, the Federal government is transferring many financial obligations to the states, and colleges and universities must compete with other—some would argue more pressing—demands on the public purse, including law enforcement, economic development, and social services.

As appropriations decline (as least as a share of all income to public institutions) enrollment demand is rising. In part, this is a response to the increasing cost of attending private institutions, but it probably also reflects the relative accessibility of many public institutions to major population centers, their resulting attractiveness to part-time, adult students, and the diverse program mix found particularly in public two-year colleges.

To meet student demand with declining appropriations, most public institutions are raising tuition and fees, some dramatically. Others are reducing programs, capping enrollment, and cutting personnel.

INTERPRETATION

State appropriations to public institutions range, on average, from 37 percent of total revenue for research universities to 42 percent for regional institutions. Only two-year institutions receive significant local funding, amounting, on average, to nearly 10 percent of total revenues.

STATE APPROPRIATIONS AS A PERCENT OF TOTAL CURRENT FUND REVENUES

PUBLIC

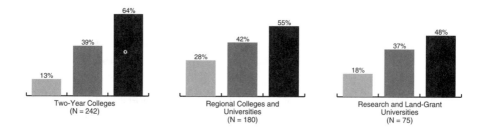

LOCAL APPROPRIATIONS AS A PERCENT OF TOTAL CURRENT FUND REVENUES

PUBLIC

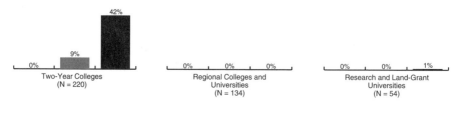

QUESTIONS FOR POLICY MAKERS TO ASK

1. What percent of our total revenues are attributable to state and local appropriations, and how does this compare with our peer institutions?

2. What have been recent trends in our receipt of state and local appropriations, and what are our prospects for the future?

3. What is the nature of our relationship with the state and locality? Are we actively working to enhance this relationship and our prospects for future funding?

4. If prospects for increased public revenues are uncertain, what other revenue sources are we developing?

Federal grants and contracts as a percent of total current fund revenues

SIGNIFICANCE

Most basic research in the United States is conducted by colleges and universities, and most of this research is funded through Federal grants and contracts. Federal funding for research and other educational activities has been growing at a slower rate in recent years, and current pressures to balance the Federal budget, largely by cutting expenditures, do not bode well for future growth in grant and contract income. The termination or reduction of agencies and programs administered by the National Endowments for the Arts and Humanities, the National Science Foundation, the U.S. Department of Education, and others will make Federal funding much more difficult to secure.

Federal grants and contracts are significant in several ways. They are sources of two kinds of income: direct support for research and other educational activities, as well as overhead income to support the larger campus infrastructure. They enable institutions to pursue their research and public service missions. And they raise the profile of the institution beyond the campus, enabling it to attract support and students nationally and internationally.

Colleges and universities are attempting to compensate for shortfalls in Federal research funding by seeking grants and contracts from corporations and foundations and by supporting research with institutional funds. Neither of these goals will be easy to achieve. Like government, corporations and foundations are besieged with competing claims for their resources. Meanwhile, institutional funds for research and related activities are scarce because institutions themselves are experiencing serious financial shortfalls.

INTERPRETATION

Federal grants and contracts figure in the revenues of all types of institutions and account, on average, for approximately 8 percent of total revenue. Revenues from this source are highest among public two-year and research universities and lowest among mid to higher priced private colleges and universities.

FEDERAL GRANTS AND CONTRACTS AS A PERCENT OF TOTAL CURRENT FUND REVENUES

PUBLIC

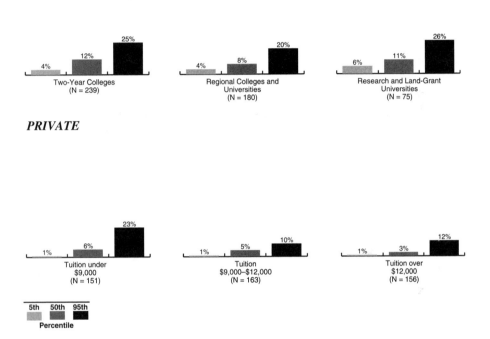

PRIVATE

QUESTIONS FOR POLICY MAKERS TO ASK

1. What percent of our total revenue is attributable to federal grants and contracts, and how does this compare with our peer institutions?

2. Have federal grants and contracts increased or decreased in recent years?

3. How much of federal grant and contract revenues are attributable to indirect cost recovery? Do these collections approximate our full average costs?

4. Are corporations or the institution itself funding more research than previously?

5. What are our plans to fund research in the future if revenues from federal grants or contracts stagnate or decline?

Private gifts, grants, and contracts as a percent of total current fund revenues

SIGNIFICANCE

Private gifts, grants, and contracts represent all revenues from private sources—e.g., individuals, foundations, corporations, churches—expended on operations. While this is a relatively minor portion of total income for most institutions, it is an important source of diversity and stability in the revenue structure. For example, income from private sources can help colleges and universities weather losses in government appropriations and tuition income, fund innovations that ultimately will enhance the institution's productivity, and provide a cushion while restructuring takes place. In addition, private support serves as a form of imprimatur for the institution's character and contributions, which in turn can garner more support. A major foundation grant can lead to other grants, just as reliable (even if modest) support from a sponsoring denomination proclaims its special relationship with a church related college, thereby bolstering student enrollment from the denomination.

It is unlikely that private support could ever compensate entirely for substantial losses of government grants and appropriations, or allow colleges and universities to lower tuition significantly or vastly increase financial aid, but even modest increases can provide important tangible and symbolic assistance.

INTERPRETATION

Private gifts, grants, and contracts represent, on average, about 4 percent of total revenue for all institutions. Revenues from these sources are substantially greater among private institutions than public colleges and universities, which began raising private money only relatively recently. Low-tuition private colleges receive more than 10 percent of their revenues via private gifts, grants, and contracts, a much higher proportion than any other type of institution, private or public.

PRIVATE GIFTS, GRANTS, AND CONTRACTS AS A PERCENT OF TOTAL CURRENT FUND REVENUES

PUBLIC

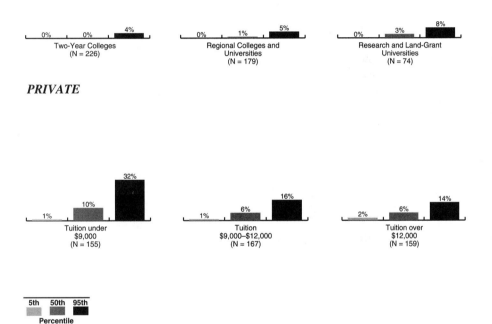

PRIVATE

5th 50th 95th
Percentile

QUESTIONS FOR POLICY MAKERS TO ASK

1. What percent of our total revenue comes from private gifts, grants, and contracts, and how does this compare with our peer institutions?

2. What specifically are our sources of private revenue, and what trends have been evident in recent years in receipt of revenues from each source?

3. What are our plans for increasing private revenue in the future?

Endowment support for operations as a percent of total current fund revenues

SIGNIFICANCE

Colleges and universities typically spend most of their expendable endowment return on current operations, although endowment support represents a very small proportion of current fund revenues for most institutions. There are three forms of endowment: pure (provided by a donor, with the proviso that the corpus will remain intact in perpetuity); term (provided by a donor, with the proviso that the corpus will remain intact for a specified period); and quasi (designated by the governing board, usually from an operating surplus, with no permanent restriction on the use of the corpus or the income). Income from pure and term endowment is usually restricted by donors to a particular purpose.

The amount of endowment to be expended each year is determined by the "spending policy" set by the governing board. Theoretically, the policy aims to approximate the portion of the endowment that can be consumed without eroding capital. However, the matter of how conservatively to define what portion of the endowment can legitimately be spent is a matter of considerable controversy. Ideally, spending policy should balance current and future financial needs of an institution, though doing so is a challenge for many boards in the current financial climate. For example, if the physical plant is crumbling and enrollment is declining for lack of financial aid funds, is a board wise to set a generous spending policy, even at the risk of eroding the value of the corpus? Or is the board's obligation to maintain the value of the endowment for future generations, even at the risk of handicapping the institution today?

INTERPRETATION

Endowment provides relatively little support for operations, especially in public institutions, which tend to have very small endowments, if they have them at all. Among private colleges and universities, endowment support represents between 2 and 4 percent of total revenues. High-tuition private institutions, which also tend to have larger endowments, report the highest percentage of total operating revenues coming from endowment. Among the average public institution, none receives significant operating revenue from endowment.

ENDOWMENT SUPPORT FOR OPERATIONS AS A PERCENT OF TOTAL CURRENT FUND REVENUES

PUBLIC

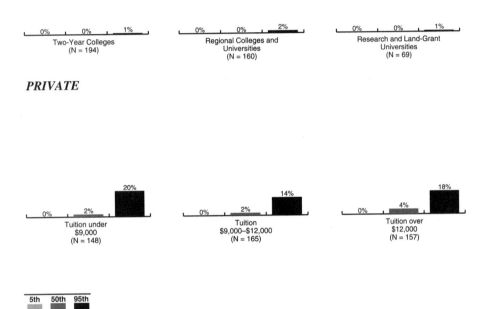

PRIVATE

5th 50th 95th
Percentile

QUESTIONS FOR POLICY MAKERS TO ASK

1. What percent of our total operating revenue is accounted for by endowment, and how does this compare with our peer institutions?

2. What specific combination of factors explains our current level of endowment support? The size of our endowment? Management results? Our spending policy?

3. How do we weigh current needs for endowment support against the desire to maintain and increase the endowment to meet the needs of future generations of students?

Sales and services of auxiliary enterprises as a percent of total current fund revenues

SIGNIFICANCE

Auxiliary enterprises exist to furnish a supplementary service to students, faculty, and staff, and they charge a fee that is directly related to, though not necessarily equal to, the cost of providing the service. Examples include residence halls, dining services, student health services, and bookstores. As a general rule, institutions should ensure that auxiliaries are not losing money. More frequently, in fact, auxiliary services are becoming an important source of net revenue for many institutions, whether through profitable management by the institution or through outsourcing.

For some institutions, making a profit on auxiliary services raises an ethical dilemma. Is it fair, for example, for a student who lives in a residence hall and eats in a campus dining room to subsidize through excess fees the education of a commuting student? Should students and faculty be charged more than necessary for books in the campus store in order to provide net revenues for the institution to spend on other activities? In some respects, the issue of "profit" on auxiliary services is a microcosm of the larger issue of cost shifting that features so prominently in consideration of tuition policies that charge more to some students in order to provide financial aid to others.

INTERPRETATION

On average, auxiliary services provide between 11 and 16 percent of total revenues across all types of institutions, public and private, with the exception of two-year public colleges, whose income from auxiliaries is approximately a third to a half that of other types of institutions. This is not surprising, given that relatively few community colleges are residential, so income from dormitories and dining halls would be expected to be far less in such institutions.

The chart on page 16, which shows expenditures for auxiliary enterprises, in combination with the data presented here, shows an excess of revenues over expenditures of approximately 4 percent. That is, for example, the average high-tuition private college earns more than 16 percent of its revenues from auxiliaries while devoting just under 13 percent of its expenditures to this area. A similar pattern is evident among the low and mid-tuition groups. Assuming a balanced budget, this means that the average private institution is netting significant income from its auxiliary enterprises. Among public institutions, revenue and expenditure levels are closer, and in the case of regional institutions and research universities, expenses outstrip revenues slightly.

SALES AND SERVICES OF AUXILIARY ENTERPRISES AS A PERCENT OF TOTAL CURRENT FUND REVENUES

PUBLIC

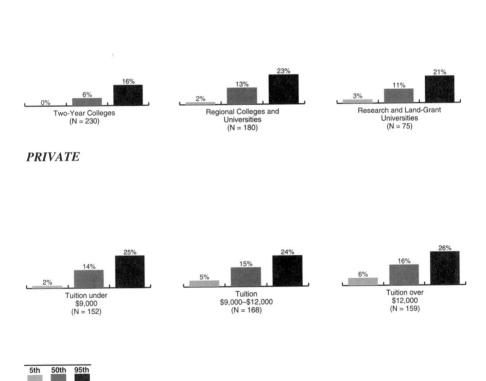

PRIVATE

QUESTIONS FOR POLICY MAKERS TO ASK

1. What percent of our total revenue is attributable to auxiliary services, and how does this compare with our peer institutions?

2. What is our philosophy regarding whether auxiliaries should break even or net a profit that can be used to subsidize other operating expenses?

3. Are our auxiliary services, individually and collectively, making money, breaking even, or running a deficit? How does this performance comport with the institution's philosophy about the purposes of auxiliary enterprises?

Sources of revenue for sponsored research

SIGNIFICANCE

These indicators reflect the extent to which institutions that receive revenues to finance research obtain them from the federal government, state and local governments, corporations, and the institution itself.

The ability to attract federal funds is a function of the institution's research priorities and capabilities and the extent to which they are consistent with federal needs and programs. Federal funding for research and other educational activities has been growing at a slower rate in recent years, and current pressures to balance the Federal budget, largely by cutting expenditures, do not bode well for future growth in grant and contract income. The termination or reduction of agencies and programs administered by the National Endowments for the Arts and Humanities, the National Science Foundation, the U.S. Department of Education, and others will make Federal funding much more difficult to secure.

Federal research monies have typically gone to a relatively few large research universities that are especially experienced and adept at competing for funds through federal peer review processes. As a result, some universities have begun to use their political clout to seek earmarked research funding though the legislative appropriations process.

State and local funding typically reflect governmental program priorities as much as institutional initiative and performance. Corporate funding depends on developing close ties with industry. Direct institutional funding usually represents only a small fraction of research support (so-called "departmental research" is included in the instructional expense category). However, the amount of direct institutional support for research may grow as institutions become more accountable for the separate costing of instruction and research.

INTERPRETATION

Most funding for sponsored research in all types of institutions comes from the federal government, amounting to between one-half and three-quarters of all sponsored research funding in all institutional categories except two-year public colleges. Among public institutions, state government is also a significant provider of research dollars.

Corporations support some research as well, accounting for 18 percent of receipts at two-year public colleges and much lower percentages in other types of institutions. In some institutional categories, including two-year publics, public research universities, and low-tuition private colleges, institutional funds account for 10 or more percent of all sponsored research revenues.

SOURCES OF REVENUE FOR SPONSORED RESEARCH

PUBLIC

Source	Public Two-year	Public Regional Colleges and Universities	Public Research and Land-Grant Universities
US government	44%	52%	60%
State and local government	18%	25%	14%
US corporations	18%	5%	5%
Private US foundations	2%	5%	2%
Bequests and gifts from living individuals	1%	1%	1%
Foreign governments, private foundations, and corporations	0%	0%	1%
Other outside sponsors	6%	5%	6%
Institutional funds	12%	7%	10%

PRIVATE

Source	Private tuition under $9,000	Private tuition $9,000–$12,000	Private tuition over $12,000
US government	63%	77%	70%
State and local government	8%	5%	6%
US corporations	4%	10%	7%
Private US foundations	13%	2%	6%
Bequests and gifts from living individuals	1%	1%	0%
Foreign governments, private foundations, and corporations	0%	0%	0%
Other outside sponsors	0%	1%	5%
Institutional funds	11%	3%	5%

A note about these tables: Numbers used in these tables are means (the numerical average), in contrast to medians (the middle value in a distribution), which are used elsewhere in this book. In a perfectly normal distribution, the median and mean are the same. Where a distribution is highly skewed, the two values may be very different.

QUESTIONS FOR POLICY MAKERS TO ASK

1. Does our institution receive external support for research? Do we use institutional funds to support research? If so, what have been the recent trends in our receipt and expenditure of these funds?

2. What proportion of our revenues for sponsored research comes from various sources? Have these proportions changed over time?

3. What accounts for any changes we have experienced in recent years in our ability to compete successfully for research dollars?

4. What are our long-term prospects for receiving research funding in the future?

Overall expenditure structure

SIGNIFICANCE

The expenditure structure reflects how an institution uses its funds to purchase goods and services to support current operations. While the same expenditure categories are used by virtually all institutions, patterns of expenditure vary among types of institutions, based largely on institutional mission, wealth, and control (public versus private). Changes in an institution's expenditure structure over time can signal growing financial strength or vulnerability. For example, growing expenditures for financial aid may signal difficulty in attracting sufficient numbers of full-pay students. Declining expenditures for plant operations and maintenance may indicate that deferred maintenance is rising. Growing expenditures for instruction in combination with declining expenditures for academic and institutional support may suggest that the institution is cutting administrative positions either to hire new faculty or to increase faculty salaries.

INTERPRETATION

Across all institutional categories, the largest item of expenditure is instruction, which accounts for between a quarter and a third of expenses among all institutions except two-year public colleges. Two-year publics devote more than 40 percent of their expenditures to instruction. Other major expenditure categories include institutional support, which comprises general administration and areas such as public relations and development; scholarships and fellowships; auxiliary services; student services; and plant operations and maintenance.

EXPENDITURE STRUCTURE

Source	Public Two-year	Public Regional Colleges and Universities	Public Research and Land-Grant Universities	Private tuition under $9,000	Private tuition $9,000– $12,000	Private tuition over $12,000
Instruction	40.8	35.7	30.2	27.1	26.1	26.3
Sponsored research	0.1	1.5	12.3	0.5	1.1	1.8
Public service	2.0	2.7	5.7	0.9	0.9	0.9
Academic support	6.9	7.5	7.5	5.8	5.6	6.1
Libraries[1]	2.3	3	2.6	2.3	2.2	2.7
Computers[1]	1.6	1	1.4	0.8	1.3	0.8
Student services	8.3	6.4	4.1	9.3	9	7.8
Institutional support	13.1	9.8	7	15.5	13.9	12
Plant operations	8.3	7.6	5.9	7.5	6.9	6.6
Scholarships and fellowships	11.6	10.2	7	19.5	20.6	19.9
Institutional scholarships and fellowships[2]	1.2	2.1	2.1	9.9	13.8	16
Mandatory transfers	0.7	1.8	1	1.9	1.8	1.7
Auxiliary enterprises	6.6	13.7	11.7	10.2	11.6	12.9
Hospitals	—	0	7.2	0	0.4	1.2
Independent operations	0.1	0.1	0.1	1	0.3	0.7
Other	1.5	3	.3	.8	1.8	2.1

Notes: Numbers used in this table are means (the numerical average), in contrast to medians (the middle value in a distribution), which are used elsewhere in this book. In a perfectly normal distribution, the median and mean are the same. Where a distribution is highly skewed, the two values may be very different. Hence, the reader will note differences between the values in this table and those found on succeeding pages, where medians of some of the same variables are displayed and described.

[1]Included in academic support.
[2]Included in scholarships.

QUESTIONS FOR POLICY MAKERS TO ASK

1. What are our most significant categories of expenditure, and how do they compare with our peer institutions?

2. How has our expenditure structure changed over recent years? Have changes been part of a conscious plan to put more resources into certain areas and to lessen support for others?

3. Which expenditure categories are likely to increase or decrease over the next few years? How are we preparing for these changes?

4. Are we identifying ways to curtail expenditures or expenditure growth?

Instructional expenditures as a percent of total current fund expenditures
Instructional expenditures per FTE student

SIGNIFICANCE

Instructional expenditures include those for credit and noncredit instruction. Also included in this category are departmental (as opposed to sponsored) research and public service that is not separately budgeted. For most institutions, the bulk of instructional expenses are for faculty salaries and benefits. As such, these expenditures reflect an investment in what for most institutions is the core mission, that of educating students. Thus, instructional expenditures often are viewed as a proxy for academic quality: They are higher in institutions where faculty are better paid, classes are smaller, and support is provided for departmental research and public service.

Instructional expenditures as a percent of total current fund expenditures is a measure of an institution's emphasis on academic versus non-academic pursuits. As colleges and universities become more complex, and as competition for students and resources increases, many institutions are spending more of their resources in areas such as fund-raising, public relations, and admissions and correspondingly less on academic pursuits. Other institutions, in an effort to preserve the academic core at any price, are cutting expenditures in other areas, thereby driving up the percentage of resources devoted to instruction.

Instructional expenditures per student may be excessive at some institutions because enrollment declines have not been matched with cuts in faculty costs, faculty salaries have been raised beyond the institution's capacity to support them, or because student-faculty ratios have been kept unnecessarily low.

INTERPRETATION

On average, private institutions devote slightly more than one-quarter of all expenditures to instruction. Among public institutions, the lowest proportion of expenditures for instruction (31 percent) is seen among research universities and the highest (42 percent) in public two-year colleges.

Public research universities and higher priced private institutions have, on average, the highest instructional expenditures per FTE student. Two-year publics and lower priced private institutions generally spend the least per FTE student. These findings are consistent with the perception that institutions with more resources—such as higher prestige public universities and higher-cost private institutions—spend relatively more in the core area of instruction. At public institutions, this reflects the greater ability of higher prestige institutions to attract both appropriations and tuition dollars. Among private institutions, it suggests that those that charge more—most of which also have higher endowments and more successful fund-raising programs—are able to spend more on instruction. These data do not show whether higher instructional expenditures are due to higher faculty salaries, smaller classes, greater support for non-teaching functions such as departmental research and public service, or some combination of those factors.

INSTRUCTIONAL EXPENDITURES AS A PERCENT OF TOTAL CURRENT FUND EXPENDITURES

PUBLIC

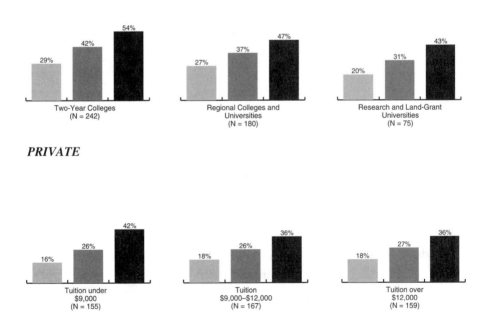

PRIVATE

INSTRUCTIONAL EXPENDITURES PER FTE STUDENT

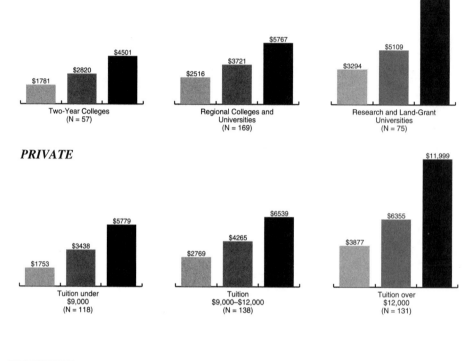

PUBLIC

Two-Year Colleges (N = 57): $1781, $2820, $4501

Regional Colleges and Universities (N = 169): $2516, $3721, $5767

Research and Land-Grant Universities (N = 75): $3294, $5109, $10,194

PRIVATE

Tuition under $9,000 (N = 118): $1753, $3438, $5779

Tuition $9,000–$12,000 (N = 138): $2769, $4265, $6539

Tuition over $12,000 (N = 131): $3877, $6355, $11,999

5th   50th   95th
Percentile

QUESTIONS FOR POLICY MAKERS TO ASK

1. What are our instructional expenditures as a percentage of total expenditures and per FTE student, and how do they compare with our peer institutions?

2. What accounts for the trends in our instructional expenditures? That is, how do they relate to enrollment changes, increases in faculty costs, changes in class size, and other factors?

3. Do we spend enough in the instructional area? If more resources were available to the institution, would we invest them in instruction or in other areas?

4. What evidence do we have that our instructional expenditures are cost effective? That is, how do we measure academic quality, and how does our quality relate to our expenditures?

5. Are we exploring ways, such as increased use of technology, reliance on part-time faculty, or other devices, to increase our efficiency in this area while maintaining quality at an acceptable level?

Academic support expenditures as a percent of total current fund expenditures

SIGNIFICANCE

Academic support expenditures sustain services that are integral to the institution's primary mission of instruction, research, and public service. They include libraries, academic computing, academic administration, educational media, museums, curriculum development, and similar key activities.

Expenditures for academic support are a significant reflection of academic quality, but, ironically, in an effort to protect the academic core (expressed in most cases as faculty positions), many institutions are either cutting academic support or allocating it a decreasing share of resources. At many colleges and universities faced with increased competition for students and resources, academic support is a third-level priority after instruction and non-academic expenditures such as fund-raising, public relations, and admissions that hold promise for a more immediate return on investment.

INTERPRETATION

Private institutions devote between 5 and 6 percent of their total expenditures to academic support, while public institutions average 7 percent.

ACADEMIC SUPPORT EXPENDITURES AS A PERCENT OF TOTAL CURRENT FUND EXPENDITURES

PUBLIC

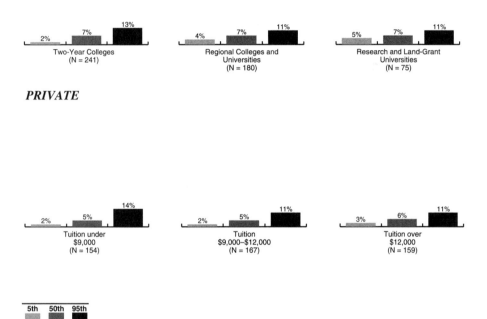

PRIVATE

5th   50th   95th
Percentile

QUESTIONS FOR POLICY MAKERS TO ASK

1. What percent of current expenditures is dedicated to academic support, and how does this compare with our peer institutions?

2. Has this percentage increased or decreased in recent years, and why?

3. Is there evidence that we are spending too much or too little in this area? Are users satisfied with the amount and quality of services?

4. What is the relationship between our academic goals and what we spend on academic support?

Excess (deficit) of current fund revenues over current fund expenditures
Current fund balance 94-95 as a percent of current fund balance 93-94

SIGNIFICANCE

Current funds are those available to support ongoing operations, as opposed, for example, to endowment or plant funds, which are restricted to longer term purposes. An operating excess generally indicates that an institution is meeting its budgetary goals and living within its means, though it does not reflect the degree to which a college or university is meeting its educational goals, nor the extent to which it is balancing its operating budget by starving programs, deferring maintenance, or taking other actions that may affect the institution's long-term future. Changes in the current fund balance from one year to the next show whether deficits are idiosyncratic or chronic.

An operating surplus may result from conscious efforts by an institution to retain a portion of operating revenue for use in future years or to convert current funds to capital, for example, by moving them to the plant fund or treating them as quasi-endowment. An operating deficit may indicate that an institution has been unable to achieve its budgetary objectives. This may be attributable to an unexpected shortfall in revenue, an unexpected increase in costs, or an ineffective budgetary process, notably poor controls and budget monitoring. An operating deficit may also be planned to allow "investments" intended to improve the quality of present programs or to start new ones.

These indicators are not applicable to some public institutions, which are prohibited from running deficits or accumulating reserves.

INTERPRETATION

On average, all types of institutions ran operating surpluses of around 2 percent during the 1994-95 fiscal year. Current fund balances increased by about 7 percent from 1994 to 1995, with the largest increases seen among public institutions, particularly research universities.

EXCESS (DEFICIT) OF CURRENT FUND REVENUES OVER CURENT FUND EXPENDITURES

PUBLIC

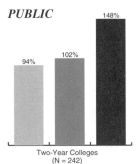

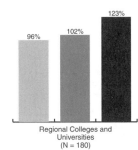

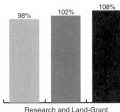

Two-Year Colleges	Regional Colleges and	Research and Land-Grant
(N = 242)	Universities	Universities
	(N = 180)	(N = 75)

PRIVATE

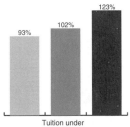

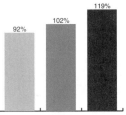

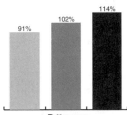

Tuition under	Tuition	Tuition over
$9,000	$9,000–$12,000	$12,000
(N = 155)	(N = 168)	(N = 159)

5th   50th   95th
Percentile

CURRENT FUND BALANCE 94-95 AS A PERCENT OF CURRENT FUND BALANCE 93-94

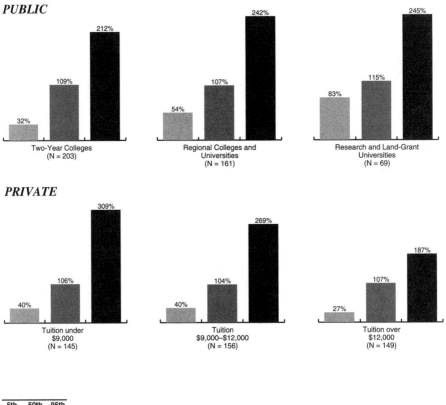

PUBLIC

Two-Year Colleges (N = 203): 32%, 109%, 212%	Regional Colleges and Universities (N = 161): 54%, 107%, 242%	Research and Land-Grant Universities (N = 69): 83%, 115%, 245%

PRIVATE

Tuition under $9,000 (N = 145): 40%, 106%, 309%	Tuition $9,000–$12,000 (N = 156): 40%, 104%, 269%	Tuition over $12,000 (N = 149): 27%, 107%, 187%

5th   50th   95th
Percentile

QUESTIONS FOR POLICY MAKERS TO ASK

1. What is our operating surplus (deficit), and how does it compare with our peer institutions?

2. Was the surplus (deficit) planned or a surprise? What will we do with a surplus? How will we manage a deficit?

3. What have been recent trends in our current fund balances, and how do they compare with our peer institutions?

4. Have we been balancing the budget by deferring expenditures in areas such as salaries, technology, or plant maintenance? If so, what plans do we have to compensate for the deferral?

Long-term debt as a percent of total liabilities

SIGNIFICANCE

Generally, long-term debt is used to finance construction and renovation of buildings or other capital projects. Short-term debt is used to finance current activities, for example, to pay immediate obligations prior to receipt of next semester's tuition payments. Debt is not inherently good or bad. For example, it may be more prudent to borrow than to use all of an institution's reserves to renovate a building, because emergencies could arise that require use of some of those funds. Moreover, it may be possible to borrow funds cheaply enough that the institution would be better off leaving its reserves invested.

On the other hand, using debt of long duration to finance current operations is nearly always a sign of severe financial stress, since it suggests a persistent inability to live within the institution's means. Moreover, even when used for legitimate purposes, too much long-term debt may limit an institution's ability to borrow for new projects in the future and may raise the cost of capital for other activities.

This indicator is not applicable to some public institutions, which are prohibited from incurring debt.

INTERPRETATION

Among all types of institutions except two-year public colleges, approximately one-half to two-thirds of all debt is long-term. Within the private college group, the proportion of long-term debt rises steadily with increases in tuition, suggesting lesser need for debt to support current activities and greater debt capacity among these relatively wealthier institutions.

In the case of two-year public colleges, only about one-fifth of debt is long-term, suggesting a relatively greater need for funds to support current activities. It is important to note, however, that this indicator does not reflect the dollar amount of debt or liabilities, and, given limitations on the ability of most public institutions to assume debt, the actual magnitude of short-term debt two-year colleges have assumed may be very low.

LONG-TERM DEBT AS A PERCENT OF TOTAL LIABILITIES

PUBLIC

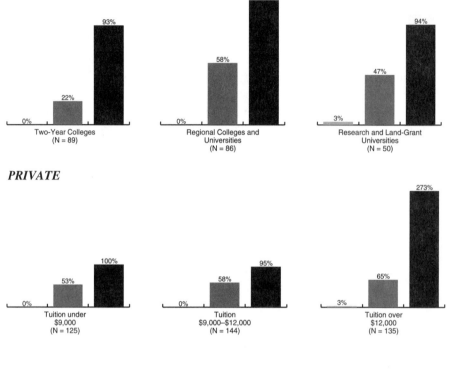

PRIVATE

5th   50th   95th
Percentile

QUESTIONS FOR POLICY MAKERS TO ASK

1. What is our proportion of long-term debt to total liabilities, and how does it compare with our peer institutions?

2. For what purposes have we incurred long-term and short-term debt? Have we assumed any long-term debt to finance short-term needs?

3. What is our debt capacity? Do we have a debt policy?

4. How do we plan to finance capital projects in the future? What role will debt play?

Total assets as a percent of total liabilities

SIGNIFICANCE

Assets are the tangible wealth of an institution, including, for example, cash, investments, inventories, receivables, land, buildings, and equipment. Liabilities are the accumulated total, for all fund groups, of obligations such as accounts payable, indebtedness, and amounts due to other fund groups. The ratio of assets to liabilities indicates the extent to which the institution has sufficient wealth to offset its obligations. Generally, the higher the ratio of assets to liabilities, the more affluent an institution is. This figure can be deceptive, however, since the physical plant represents the largest portion of assets owned by most institutions, but in most instances plant cannot be readily converted to cash. Moreover, plant ownership obligates an institution to recurring expenditures in areas such as maintenance and replacement.

Liabilities must eventually be retired, generally from current revenue, gifts, or other revenue in-flows. If these are not adequate, assets must be disposed of to meet debt payments.

INTERPRETATION

On average, across all types of institutions, assets exceed liabilities by a factor of five to one. The ratio is higher for public institutions, most likely because they have financed some capital projects through appropriations rather than borrowing. Among private institutions, the asset-to-liability ratio is highest within the high-tuition group, another indication of the relatively stronger financial position of these wealthier institutions.

TOTAL ASSETS AS A PERCENT OF TOTAL LIABILITIES

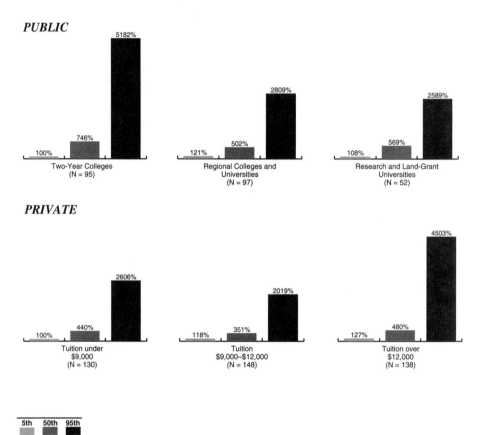

PUBLIC

Two-Year Colleges (N = 95): 100%, 746%, 5182%

Regional Colleges and Universities (N = 97): 121%, 502%, 2809%

Research and Land-Grant Universities (N = 52): 108%, 569%, 2589%

PRIVATE

Tuition under $9,000 (N = 130): 100%, 440%, 2606%

Tuition $9,000–$12,000 (N = 148): 118%, 351%, 2019%

Tuition over $12,000 (N = 138): 127%, 480%, 4503%

5th 50th 95th Percentile

QUESTIONS FOR POLICY MAKERS TO ASK

1. What is our asset-to-liability ratio, and how does it compare with our peer institutions?

2. How has this ratio changed over time, and what explains the changes?

3. What is the composition of our assets and liabilities?

4. How liquid are our assets? How comfortable are we that our liabilities are manageable and appropriate, given our institution's plans and resources?

Market value of endowment as a percent of total assets
Market value of endowment per FTE student

SIGNIFICANCE

In many respects, endowment is the most desirable of institutional assets because, even when restricted to a particular use, it is more flexible and less expensive to maintain than plant, the chief asset of most institutions. There are three forms of endowment: pure (provided by a donor, with the proviso that the corpus will remain intact in perpetuity) term (provided by a donor, with the proviso that the corpus will remain intact for a specified period), and quasi (designated by the governing board, with no permanent restriction on use of the corpus or the income). Income from pure and term endowment is usually restricted by donors to a particular purpose.

Endowment income allows an institution to invest in new programs and to improve the quality of existing offerings. It also provides greater flexibility in the use of other current funds, to the extent, for example, that it funds student aid or pays faculty salaries that otherwise would have to be financed with tuition or other revenues. Furthermore, income from endowment can shield an institution from some of the vagaries of the marketplace, for example, by compensating for an unexpected enrollment downturn.

Endowment market value as a percent of total assets distinguishes the value of endowment from other assets such as plant, which usually are less flexible. The market value of endowment per FTE student reflects relative wealth, taking into account differences in institutional size.

INTERPRETATION

Endowment represents more than one-third of all institutional assets in the private sector, with the highest proportion seen in the highest tuition group. This indicates that, not only are high-tuition institutions wealthier overall, but a greater portion of their wealth is in the form of endowment rather than plant or other assets. Public institutions often have few, if any, endowment assets, so it is not surprising that endowment represents only about 4 percent of the total assets of public colleges and universities. The percentage is highest among research universities, which are those most likely to have substantial endowments.

Endowment per FTE student is highest by far among the high-tuition private group, nearly $22,000—approximately three times the magnitude seen in the low and mid-tuition groups. This indicates that higher cost institutions have more endowment on a per-student basis—and hence more endowment income—to support current expenditures.

MARKET VALUE OF ENDOWMENT AS A PERCENT OF TOTAL ASSETS

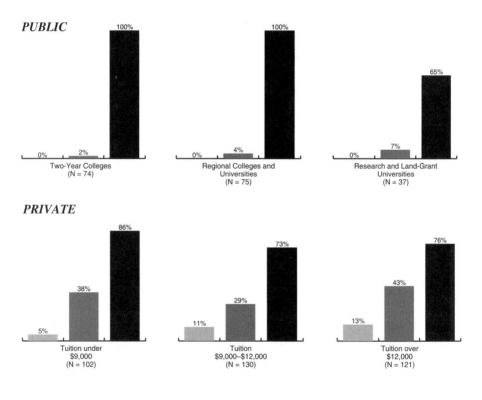

MARKET VALUE OF ENDOWMENT PER FTE STUDENT

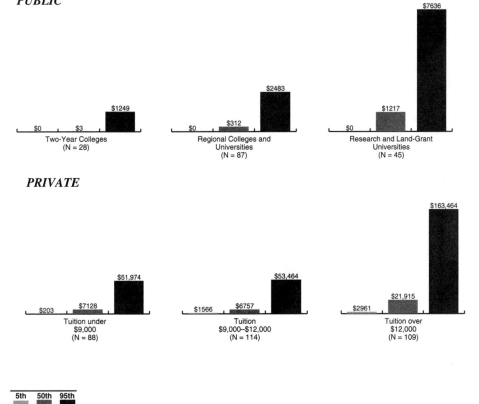

PUBLIC

PRIVATE

5th 50th 95th
Percentile

QUESTIONS FOR POLICY MAKERS TO ASK

1. What is the size of our endowment, and how does it compare with peer institutions?

2. Do we have a target size for the endowment? Is this target realistic given our fund-raising capacity, spending policy, and endowment performance?

3. Do we have a specific plan for increasing, maintaining, or (if necessary) decreasing our endowment, or are these changes unintentional?

Yield as a percent of total endowment
Total return as a percent of total endowment
End-of-year market value of total endowment as a percent of beginning-of-year value

SIGNIFICANCE

Endowment yield is the return—dividends and interest—earned on the endowment (pure, term, and quasi) during the year and available for expenditure. In part, it is a measure of how well the endowment has been managed. However, yield does not reflect appreciation of assets, and a lower yield may be offset by an increase in appreciation of the endowment or by the prospect of future gains.

Total return on endowment includes yield plus appreciation (or depreciation) of endowment assets. Endowments with lower yields sometimes have higher appreciation. Generally, the higher the total return, the better the endowment is performing. However, lower total return may reflect an investment strategy designed to produce greater future income and appreciation. This strategy may carry a high risk of capital loss.

In order to preserve the future purchasing power of the endowment, market value should increase over time. Increased market value occurs through the addition of new assets, as well as growth in and retention of yield and appreciation.

Some institutions spend yield and only yield to fund current operations. Others use a "payout formula" or "spending rule" that permits expenditure of a portion of appreciation, with the goal of maintaining or increasing the endowment's value over time.

INTERPRETATION

Endowment yield across all types of institutions averaged about 4.5 percent during fiscal year 1995, with the lowest yield seen in high-tuition private institutions. However, total return was highest among that same group of institutions, averaging nearly 11 percent. Similarly, among public institutions, the relatively wealthier research university group earned total returns of nearly 8 percent, which were the highest seen in the public sector.

This suggests that wealthier institutions, which are less dependent on investing for short-term yield to support current expenditures, can take the longer view of endowment growth that stresses appreciation of endowment assets. And, in fact, among private institutions, the high-tuition group experienced the greatest growth in endowment market value, up nearly 13 percent. Along the same lines, endowments in the public research university cohort grew by nearly 17 percent, also bearing out the observation that wealthier institutions are less dependent on current income from endowment and thus can invest for the long term. In addition, these endowments probably grew through addition of new gifts.

YIELD AS A PERCENT OF TOTAL ENDOWMENT

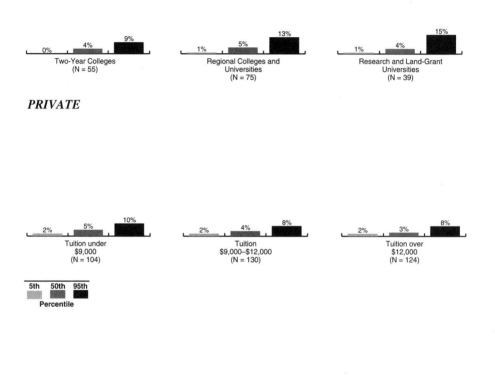

PUBLIC

Two-Year Colleges
(N = 55)

0%   4%   9%

Regional Colleges and
Universities
(N = 75)

1%   5%   13%

Research and Land-Grant
Universities
(N = 39)

1%   4%   15%

PRIVATE

Tuition under
$9,000
(N = 104)

2%   5%   10%

Tuition
$9,000–$12,000
(N = 130)

2%   4%   8%

Tuition over
$12,000
(N = 124)

2%   3%   8%

5th   50th   95th
Percentile

TOTAL RETURN AS A PERCENT OF TOTAL ENDOWMENT

PUBLIC

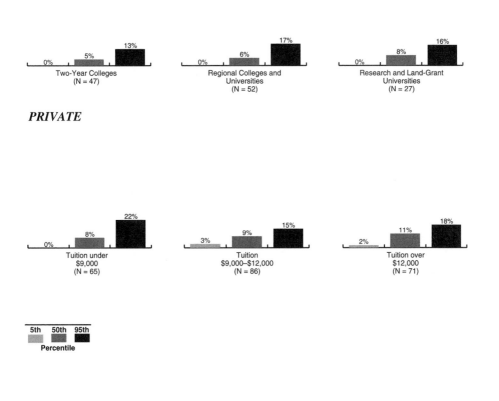

PRIVATE

END-OF-YEAR MARKET VALUE OF TOTAL ENDOWMENT AS A PERCENT OF BEGINNING-OF-YEAR VALUE

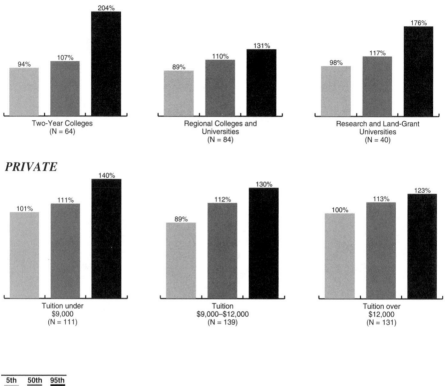

PUBLIC

Two-Year Colleges (N = 64): 94%, 107%, 204%

Regional Colleges and Universities (N = 84): 89%, 110%, 131%

Research and Land-Grant Universities (N = 40): 98%, 117%, 176%

PRIVATE

Tuition under $9,000 (N = 111): 101%, 111%, 140%

Tuition $9,000–$12,000 (N = 139): 89%, 112%, 130%

Tuition over $12,000 (N = 131): 100%, 113%, 123%

5th   50th   95th
Percentile

QUESTIONS FOR POLICY MAKERS TO ASK

1. What are our trends in endowment yield, total return, and growth, and how do they compare with peer institutions?

2. What factors underlie our yield, total return, and growth? For example, are we investing for short or long-term yield? Are we taking risks to increase the value of the endowment?

3. What is our endowment spending policy? Do we spend only yield, or do we also use a portion of appreciation? How is the growth in our

endowment affected by our spending policy? Are we consciously trying to preserve—and even increase—the purchasing power of our endowment?

4. Who manages the endowment, what instructions have managers been given, and who oversees their performance?

5. What is our investment strategy? Are we more interested in current yield or long-term performance? What level of risk are we willing to tolerate to produce the income and appreciation we believe we need?

Quasi endowment as a percent of total endowment

SIGNIFICANCE

Unlike pure and term endowment, quasi endowment is established at the option of the governing board, and neither the principal nor the yield and appreciation are legally restricted as to use. Thus, quasi endowment is the most flexible form of endowment. Because it often is constituted of current fund surpluses, quasi endowment also can be an indicator of the institution's frugality and prudence.

Like other forms of endowment, income from quasi endowment allows an institution to invest in new initiatives and enhance current offerings. Moreover, because it is unrestricted and therefore completely flexible, quasi endowment provides an especially valuable cushion against the vicissitudes of enrollments, gift income, and investment performance.

INTERPRETATION

There is a direct relationship between institutional wealth and level of quasi-endowment. That is, among public institutions, the highest proportions of quasi-endowment are found in research universities, followed by regional institutions. In the private sector, the proportion of quasi-endowment varies directly with tuition level. This suggests that institutions with more assets overall have been able to set aside more of their own resources to invest. In turn, quasi-endowment provides these institutions with the flexibility to spend corpus, yield, or appreciation in any combination they desire, for any purpose their boards designate.

QUASI ENDOWMENT AS A PERCENT OF TOTAL ENDOWMENT

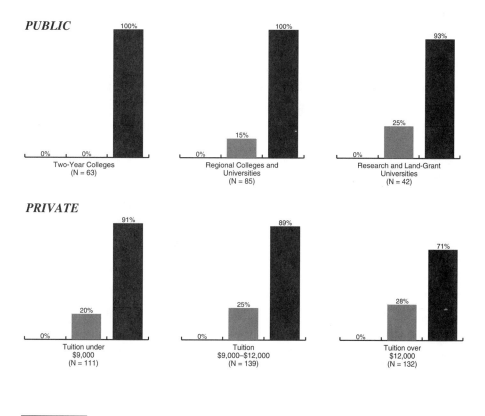

PUBLIC

Two-Year Colleges
(N = 63)

Regional Colleges and
Universities
(N = 85)

Research and Land-Grant
Universities
(N = 42)

PRIVATE

Tuition under
$9,000
(N = 111)

Tuition
$9,000–$12,000
(N = 139)

Tuition over
$12,000
(N = 132)

5th 50th 95th
Percentile

QUESTIONS FOR POLICY MAKERS TO ASK

1. What proportion of our endowment assets are quasi-endowment, and how does that compare with our peer institutions?

2. What have been our long-term trends in accumulation of quasi-endowment, and what do those trends suggest for the future?

3. What have been the sources of our quasi-endowment, and are those sources likely to provide additional assets in the future?

4. Why do we maintain quasi-endowment, and how do we use it?

Overall development structure

SIGNIFICANCE

An institution's overall development structure reflects the diversity of sources from which it receives charitable gifts. A balanced giving structure reflects a broad range of support for an institution, a multifaceted development strategy, and the likelihood of stable giving over time. If giving is from relatively few sources, and those sources are unstable or unreliable, income from gifts may be volatile. Underperformance in some giving areas also may indicate that an institution has undeveloped opportunities to increase future giving. A particularly large bequest or a capital campaign may distort the giving picture in any particular year, so it is essential to monitor multi-year trends and to be able to explain sometimes dramatic rises and drops in gift income. Moreover, institutions should take great care in deciding how to use large, nonrecurring gifts to avoid assuming long-term obligations that will necessitate continuing funding.

INTERPRETATION

Major sources of private gifts to most institutions include alumni, other individuals, private foundations, corporations, and bequests. In only a few cases are gifts from parents, fund-raising consortia, and religious organizations responsible for more than a very small fraction of total gifts.

DEVELOPMENT STRUCTURE

PUBLIC

Source	Public Two-year	Public Regional Colleges and Universities	Public Research and Land-Grant Universities
Alumni	9%	19%	24%
Parents	0%	1%	0%
Other individuals	24%	22%	16%
Private foundations	13%	12%	15%
Corporations	32%	28%	28%
Religious organizations	0%	0%	0%
Fund-raising consortia	1%	1%	0%
Other organizations	6%	10%	7%
Bequests received	16%	8%	10%

PRIVATE

Source	Private tuition under $9,000	Private tuition $9,000–$12,000	Private tuition over $12,000
Alumni	14%	23%	38%
Parents	3%	4%	3%
Other individuals	24%	24%	15%
Private foundations	19%	17%	16%
Corporations	9%	13%	10%
Religious organizations	12%	6%	1%
Fund-raising consortia	3%	1%	0%
Other organizations	4%	2%	3%
Bequests received	13%	10%	13%

A note about this table: Numbers used in this table are means (the numerical average), in contrast to medians (the middle value in a distribution), which are used elsewhere in this book. In a perfectly normal distribution, the median and mean are the same. Where a distribution is highly skewed, the two values may be very different. Hence, the reader will note differences between the values in this table and those found on succeeding pages, where medians of some of the same variables are displayed and described.

QUESTIONS FOR POLICY MAKERS TO ASK

1. What are our most significant sources of private giving, and how do they compare with our peer institutions?

2. How dependent are we on one or two single sources of gifts, and has this dependence increased or decreased over time?

3. Can we identify any new or enhanced sources of gift income? What are our plans for developing these sources?

Gifts from individuals
Gifts from alumni as a percent of total gifts
Gifts from parents as a percent of total gifts
Gifts from other individuals as a percent of total gifts
Gifts from trustees, included in the above categories, as a percent of total gifts

SIGNIFICANCE

Gifts from individuals, whether for operating or capital purposes, are an increasingly important form of institutional income, as well as a symbol of personal support for an institution, which may help a college or university in other ways. For example, an alumnus or other individual who thinks enough of a college to support it financially probably would recommend it to a prospective student as well.

Other advantages accrue to institutions that raise funds from individuals. Such gifts, especially when given to support current operations, often are unrestricted or, at most, restricted to an area such as student financial aid for which the institution actively seeks support. Exceptions include very large gifts from individuals, which often are provided to establish a particular program or project of special interest to the giver.

Colleges and universities face less competition for support from individuals, who usually are affiliated with no more than one or two institutions, than they do from corporations and other organizations, to which hundreds of institutions may turn for support. Individual giving also may serve as a form of leverage for fund raising from organizations. Some corporations are willing to match their employees' charitable gifts. Moreover, corporations and foundations that receive grant proposals from colleges and universities are rightly interested in the degree to which individuals support the institution. For instance, if its alumni and trustees, who supposedly know it best, are unwilling to support it financially, why would a corporation or foundation want to do so?

INTERPRETATION

Among both public and private colleges and universities, the wealthier and more prestigious the institution, the higher the percentage of gifts it receives from individuals. That is, public research universities receive a higher proportion of gifts from individuals than public regional institutions, which, in turn receive more than two-year colleges. Among private institutions, the higher the tuition level, the greater proportion of total giving that is provided by individuals.

Gifts from alumni rather than parents and other individuals drive this pattern, perhaps reflecting relatively greater giving capacity by graduates of more prestigious institutions, as well as greater attachment to these institutions by their graduates. In fact, as a proportion of total gift income, giving by individuals other than alumni actually falls in most cases as institutional prestige rises, suggesting that capacity and attachment of non-alumni is greater than that of alumni in lower cost and lower prestige institutions.

Gifts from trustees, including board members of public college and university foundations, are counted within the categories of alumni, parents, and other individuals, as appropriate. When broken out as a separate category, such gifts to private institutions rise, as a percentage of total giving, with institutional tuition level. This suggests relatively greater capacity and/or commitment by trustees of wealthier and more prestigious institutions. The pattern is exactly the opposite among public institutions. As institutional prestige and wealth increase, giving by governing and institutional foundation board members in the public sector decreases as a percentage of total giving.

GIFTS FROM ALUMNI AS A PERCENT OF TOTAL GIFTS

PUBLIC

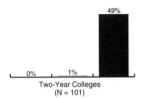

Two-Year Colleges
(N = 101)

0%   1%   49%

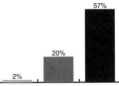

Regional Colleges and
Universities
(N = 143)

2%   20%   57%

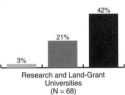

Research and Land-Grant
Universities
(N = 68)

3%   21%   42%

PRIVATE

Tuition under
$9,000
(N = 130)

1%   9%   48%

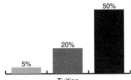

Tuition
$9,000–$12,000
(N = 160)

5%   20%   50%

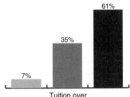

Tuition over
$12,000
(N = 148)

7%   35%   61%

5th   50th   95th
Percentile

GIFTS FROM PARENTS AS A PERCENT OF TOTAL GIFTS

PUBLIC

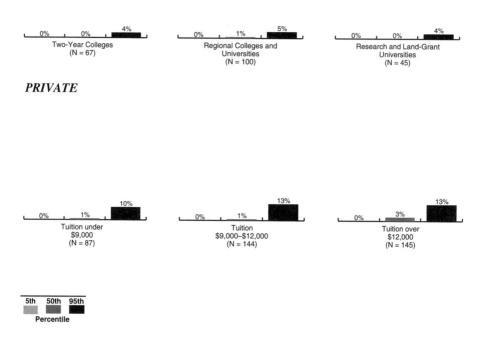

	0%	0%	4%
	Two-Year Colleges (N = 67)		

	0%	1%	5%
	Regional Colleges and Universities (N = 100)		

	0%	0%	4%
	Research and Land-Grant Universities (N = 45)		

PRIVATE

	0%	1%	10%
	Tuition under $9,000 (N = 87)		

	0%	1%	13%
	Tuition $9,000–$12,000 (N = 144)		

	0%	3%	13%
	Tuition over $12,000 (N = 145)		

5th	50th	95th
Percentile

GIFTS FROM OTHER INDIVIDUALS AS A PERCENT OF TOTAL GIFTS

PUBLIC

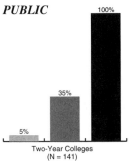

Two-Year Colleges
(N = 141)

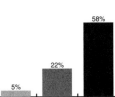

Regional Colleges and
Universities
(N = 142)

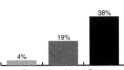

Research and Land-Grant
Universities
(N = 65)

PRIVATE

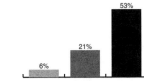

Tuition under
$9,000
(N = 129)

Tuition
$9,000–$12,000
(N = 160)

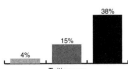

Tuition over
$12,000
(N = 148)

5th   50th   95th
Percentile

GIFTS FROM TRUSTEES, INCLUDED IN THE PREVIOUS CATEGORIES, AS A PERCENT OF TOTAL GIFTS

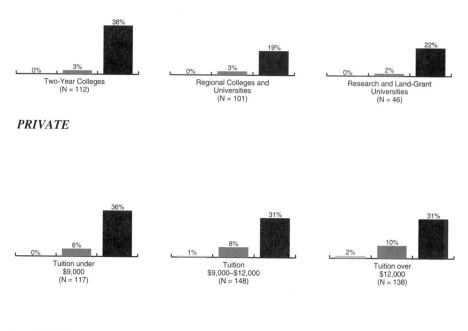

PUBLIC

38%

0%   3%

Two-Year Colleges
(N = 112)

19%

0%   3%

Regional Colleges and
Universities
(N = 101)

22%

0%   2%

Research and Land-Grant
Universities
(N = 46)

PRIVATE

36%

0%   6%

Tuition under
$9,000
(N = 117)

31%

1%   8%

Tuition
$9,000–$12,000
(N = 148)

31%

2%   10%

Tuition over
$12,000
(N = 138)

5th   50th   95th
Percentile

QUESTIONS FOR POLICY MAKERS TO ASK

1. What are our most significant sources of individual giving, and how do they compare with our peer institutions?

2. How diverse is our individual giving, and how have patterns in individual giving changed over time?

3. What are we doing to enhance our relationships with individual givers?

Gifts from organizations
Gifts from private foundations as a percent of total gifts
Gifts from corporations as a percent of total gifts
Gifts from religious organizations as a percent of total gifts
Gifts from fund-raising consortia as a percent of total gifts
Gifts from other organizations as a percent of total gifts

SIGNIFICANCE

While the largest number of gifts to an institution invariably come from individuals, the total value of gifts from organizations often can exceed the value of individual contributions. Moreover, the very large gifts needed to launch a major program or construct a building may sometimes be more readily obtained from an organization than from individuals, especially in the case of institutions whose alumni and trustees are not wealthy.

Competition for gifts from foundations and corporations is fierce, and the gifts themselves are usually restricted to particular purposes. Corporations, in particular, tend to give to institutions that offer direct or indirect benefits to them.

Increasingly, corporations and foundations are making gifts to colleges and universities contingent on an institution's ability to raise matching funds from other sources, usually individuals. This development bolsters the argument for continuous cultivation of individual givers, even as an institution seeks gifts from organizations.

INTERPRETATION

Among private institutions, the largest source of giving by organizations is private foundations, which account for approximately 14 percent of all private giving. As a percentage of total giving from all sources—individual and organizational—foundation giving decreases as tuition increases. The same pattern holds for giving by religious organizations, though this source accounts for a much smaller proportion of total giving.

Corporate giving to private institutions amounts to approximately 9 percent of overall gift receipts. This contrasts sharply with public institutions, which, overall, receive more than one-quarter of all of their gift income from corporations, a figure that rises slightly with institutional prestige and selectivity, ranging from 25 percent among community colleges to nearly 30 percent among research institutions. A similar pattern holds in foundation giving to public institutions, rising from 5 percent of gift receipts to community colleges to 14 percent among research universities.

GIFTS FROM PRIVATE FOUNDATIONS AS A PERCENT OF TOTAL GIFTS

PUBLIC

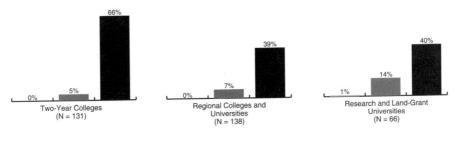

PRIVATE

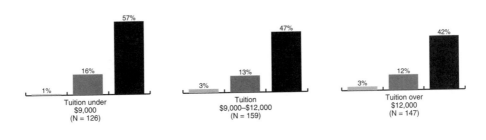

GIFTS FROM CORPORATIONS AS A PERCENT OF TOTAL GIFTS

PUBLIC

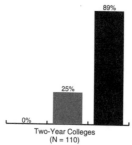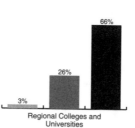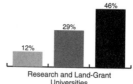

PRIVATE

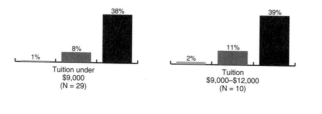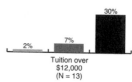

5th 50th 95th
Percentile

GIFTS FROM RELIGIOUS ORGANIZATIONS AS A PERCENT OF TOTAL GIFTS

PUBLIC

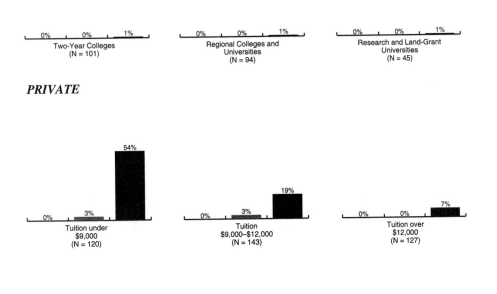

PRIVATE

5th	50th	95th
Percentile

GIFTS FROM FUND-RAISING CONSORTIA AS A PERCENT OF TOTAL GIFTS

PUBLIC

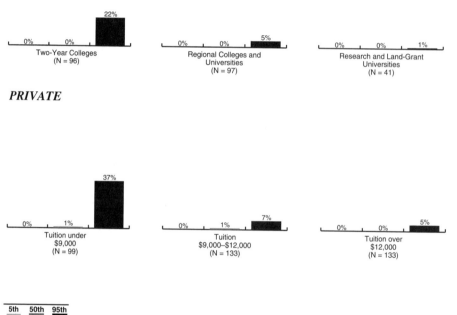

PRIVATE

5th   50th   95th
Percentile

GIFTS FROM OTHER ORGANIZATIONS AS A PERCENT OF TOTAL GIFTS

PUBLIC

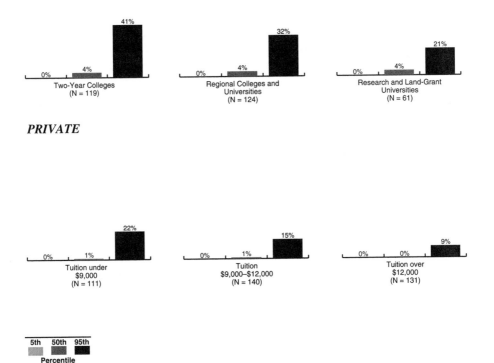

PRIVATE

QUESTIONS FOR POLICY MAKERS TO ASK

1. What are our most significant sources of giving from organizations, and how do they compare with our peer institutions?

2. How diverse is our organizational giving, and how have patterns in individual giving changed over time?

3. What are we doing to enhance our relationships with organizations that currently support us or that may become supporters in the future?

Planned giving

Bequests received as a percent of total gifts
Market value of new planned gifts as a percent of total
**   gifts actually received**
Net realizable value of new planned gifts as a percent of
**   total gifts actually received**

SIGNIFICANCE

Planned giving is a significant source of future income to many institutions, and most colleges and universities view planned gifts as one of the few potential growth areas in their fund-raising operations. Traditionally, bequests were the only form of planned gifts sought by most institutions. Today, colleges and universities are aggressively promoting an array of vehicles that enable an individual to enjoy tax benefits while providing current or future assistance to a charitable organization.

Receipt of bequests and other planned gifts tends to be uneven and unpredictable, so institutions should avoid relying on them to balance the operating budget. Moreover, securing planned gifts requires considerable technical knowledge, research, and cultivation by development staff, as well as substantial investments of time by senior officers and trustees. Institutions should track the cost-benefit relationships of these activities.

INTERPRETATION

In virtually all cases, all forms of planned giving rise, as a percentage of current giving, as institutional selectivity, wealth, and prestige increase. That is, among private institutions, bequests received rise as a percentage of total giving from under 5 percent at low-tuition colleges to nearly 10 percent at high-tuition institutions. The market value and net realizable value of new planned gifts to high-tuition institutions, proportionate to total current giving, are nearly double that of low-tuition colleges. (By definition, new planned gifts have not yet been received, and they are shown here in relation to current giving only to provide a rough estimate of their future worth, relative to other sources of support.)

Among public institutions, bequests are not a factor for community colleges, they rise to nearly 3 percent of gifts to regional universities, and they double to more than 5 percent of gifts to research universities. Neither community colleges nor regional institutions, on average, report receiving any new planned gifts, but research universities fare nearly as well on these measures as the average private institution does.

The relatively greater success of public research universities and higher tuition private colleges in attracting planned gifts probably reflects their longer experience in promoting the benefits of these sometimes esoteric vehicles to potential givers. Moreover, alumni and other supporters of more prestigious institutions may be wealthier and therefore more able to give larger sums, especially if the gifts provide tax benefits.

BEQUESTS RECEIVED AS A PERCENT OF TOTAL GIFTS

PUBLIC

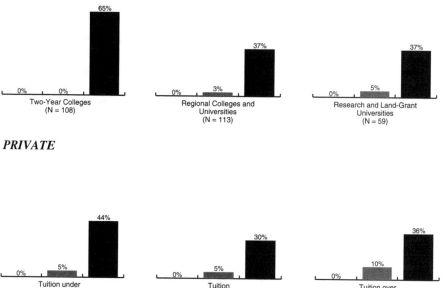

PRIVATE

5th   50th   95th
Percentile

MARKET VALUE OF NEW PLANNED GIFTS AS A PERCENT OF TOTAL GIFTS ACTUALLY RECEIVED

PUBLIC

404%	123%	47%
Two-Year Colleges (N = 90)	Regional Colleges and Universities (N = 95)	Research and Land-Grant Universities (N = 50)

PRIVATE

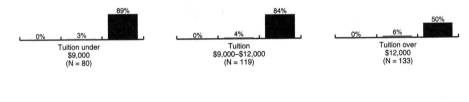

89%	84%	50%
Tuition under $9,000 (N = 80)	Tuition $9,000–$12,000 (N = 119)	Tuition over $12,000 (N = 133)

5th 50th 95th
Percentile

NET REALIZABLE VALUE OF NEW PLANNED GIFTS AS A PERCENT OF TOTAL GIFTS ACTUALLY RECEIVED

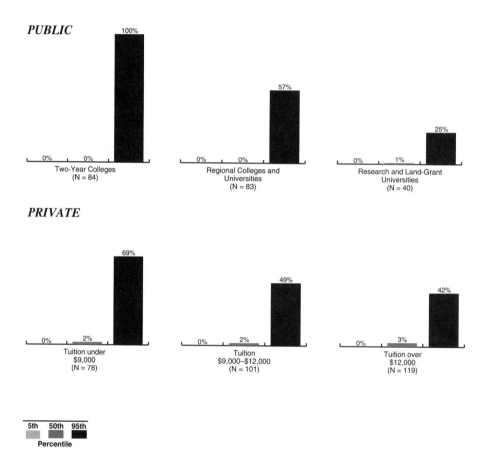

QUESTIONS FOR POLICY MAKERS TO ASK

1. What percent of our total gift income is represented by bequests, and how does this compare with our peer institutions?

2. What is the value of our new planned gifts, relative to current giving from all sources, and how does this compare with our peer institutions?

3. Are we actively involved in identifying and soliciting planned gifts?

4. How do we use income from bequests? For recurring or for non-recurring expenditures?

Percent of living alumni who have given at any time in past 5 years

SIGNIFICANCE

Alumni are a unique, select, and continuing source of support that is one of the most valuable resources any institution has. Alumni giving is important for its own sake—as a source of needed gifts—but it also serves as a proxy for confidence in an institution's performance. When alumni support an institution generously and in large numbers, the act sends an unmistakable message to other sources of funds and support that this is an institution worthy of their support as well.

INTERPRETATION

Repeating the pattern seen in other indicators of private giving, alumni participation in giving rises dramatically as institutional wealth, selectivity, and prestige increase. In the public sector, the participation rate is just 2 percent in community colleges and grows to more than 20 percent in research universities. Among private colleges and universities, 25 percent of alumni of low-tuition institutions gave in the previous five years, rising to 43 percent in high-tuition colleges.

PERCENT OF LIVING ALUMNI WHO HAVE GIVEN AT ANY TIME IN THE PAST 5 YEARS

PUBLIC

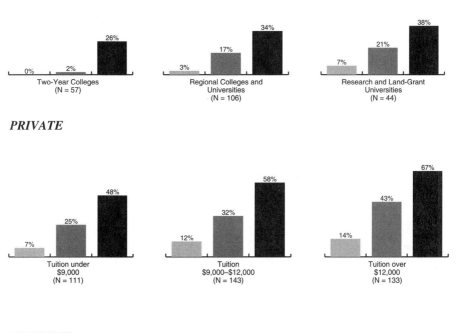

5th   50th   95th
Percentile

QUESTIONS FOR POLICY MAKERS TO ASK

1. What percent of our alumni have contributed to the institution in the past five years, and how does this compare with our peer institutions?

2. What does our level of support from alumni say about their attitudes toward the institution?

3. What are we doing to increase alumni participation in giving?

Physical Capital

Plant operations and maintenance expenditures as a percent of total current fund expenditures

SIGNIFICANCE

Expenditures for plant operations and maintenance encompass the staff and supplies used to service and maintain campus grounds and facilities that are dedicated to educational and general purposes. An appealing and well maintained campus helps attract and retain top faculty and students and helps persuade donors and other supporters that the institution is robust and viable over the long term.

Buildings and grounds are expensive to operate, and many facilities constructed since the end of World War II, when college enrollments first began to soar, are now in need of significant repair and renovation. This demand arises at a time when there are myriad competing claims on institutional budgets. Many of these claims, such as those for student financial aid, faculty salaries, and purchase of technology, seem more pressing than investments in often invisible improvements to campus infrastructure. However, failure to invest in operations and maintenance creates backlogs that become even more difficult and expensive to fund in the future.

While under-maintenance of facilities and grounds is by far the more common problem, a few institutions probably spend too much in this area and have a plant that, in light of limited resources and competing needs, is over-maintained.

INTERPRETATION

On average, institutions devote about 7 percent of their total expenditures to plant operations and maintenance. This percentage tends to fall slightly as institutional wealth and prestige rise. Because, for example, public research universities and high-tuition private colleges tend to be larger than other institutions in their respective sectors, they may be able to take advantage of economies of scale to lower their percentage of expenditures for operations and maintenance. Also, because the total expenditures of more selective and prestigious institutions are higher, they actually may spend more dollars on plant operations and maintenance than institutions with smaller budgets whose percentage of expenditures is higher.

PLANT OPERATIONS AND MAINTENANCE EXPENDITURES AS A PERCENT OF TOTAL CURRENT FUND EXPENDITURES

PUBLIC

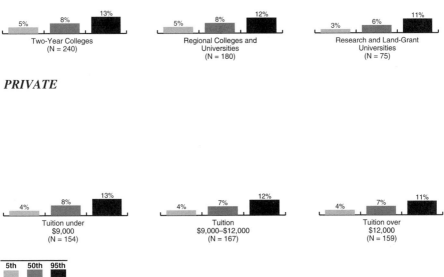

PRIVATE

5th 50th 95th
Percentile

QUESTIONS FOR POLICY MAKERS TO ASK

1. What percent of our current fund expenditures are devoted to plant operations and maintenance, and how does this compare with our peer institutions?

2. Is this amount adequate? Is it excessive? Is our level of deferred maintenance increasing or declining?

3. What have been our recent trends in allocation of funds for plant operations and maintenance, between, for example, staff and supplies, academic and non-academic facilities, and between buildings and grounds?

End-of-year replacement value of plant as a percent of beginning-of-year replacement value of plant

SIGNIFICANCE

The annual percentage increase in replacement value of plant, over and above inflation, gauges the growth of plant and plant renovations during the year. Despite overall financial shortages in higher education, many institutions continue to construct new buildings, and many others are upgrading existing facilities to meet new demands.

Additions to the value of plant are not always a sign of strong current financial condition. The gestation period between the decision to build and the completion of the building is often very long, and by the time a building is completed an institution's financial situation may have improved or deteriorated. Moreover, many institutions assume debt to construct new plant, and so plant investments may be highly leveraged.

The decision to build facilities or undertake extensive renovations is often a competitive move. Particularly among private colleges, competition for students is fierce. Having the latest in science laboratories, residential space, or recreational facilities can provide a significant competitive advantage.

Although new construction generally requires less upkeep than aging plant, new buildings add to operating and maintenance costs over time.

INTERPRETATION

On average, the replacement value of plant on all campuses increased by approximately 4.5 percent, slightly above the rate of inflation. Plant value increased more in the public sector than among private institutions, with the smallest average increase—just 3 percent—seen in high-tuition private institutions.

END-OF-YEAR REPLACEMENT VALUE OF PLANT AS A PERCENT OF BEGINNING-OF-YEAR REPLACEMENT VALUE OF PLANT

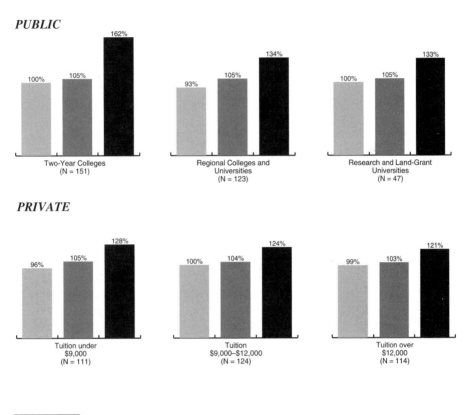

PUBLIC

Two-Year Colleges (N = 151): 100%, 105%, 162%

Regional Colleges and Universities (N = 123): 93%, 105%, 134%

Research and Land-Grant Universities (N = 47): 100%, 105%, 133%

PRIVATE

Tuition under $9,000 (N = 111): 96%, 105%, 128%

Tuition $9,000–$12,000 (N = 124): 100%, 104%, 124%

Tuition over $12,000 (N = 114): 99%, 103%, 121%

5th 50th 95th
Percentile

QUESTIONS FOR POLICY MAKERS TO ASK

1. How has the replacement value of our plant changed over the past year, and how does that change compare with our peers?

2. What accounts for trends in replacement value: New construction? Renovation? Demolition?

3. Do we have a comprehensive campus master plan that specifies future priorities for new construction, renovation, and demolition?

4. What projects are under consideration that will change the value of the plant in the future?

Estimated maintenance backlog of total plant as a percent of total replacement value of plant

SIGNIFICANCE

The cost of a building to an institution does not stop once construction has been completed. In fact, the cost of operation and maintenance over the useful life of a building often exceeds the cost of construction. During the last two decades, in particular, many institutions deferred maintenance of their buildings to reduce current expenditures and free up funds to be used in areas judged to be of higher priority. As a result, many institutions have accumulated significant deferred or unmet—and usually unfunded—maintenance. Maintenance backlog as a percent of total replacement value of plant measures the relative amount of this deferred cost.

A challenge to many institutions is to estimate this backlog accurately. Too few colleges and universities have undertaken systematic study of their deferred maintenance situation. Doing so reveals the extent of the problem, helps identify areas requiring immediate attention, and provides a starting point for financial planning to deal with the backlog.

INTERPRETATION

Many institutions did not respond to this question, suggesting that they have not systematically calculated the extent of their deferred maintenance problem. Those that did provide a non-zero response estimated their deferred maintenance backlog at around 4 percent, ranging from more than 2 percent at low-tuition private colleges to just over 7 percent at public research universities. Objective studies of deferred maintenance have estimated the average level nationally at around 7 percent of plant replacement value.

The possible unreliability of responses to this question suggests that many institutions should make a greater effort to estimate their maintenance backlog and, by extension, to plan for financing needed repairs.

ESTIMATED MAINTENANCE BACKLOG OF TOTAL PLANT AS A PERCENT OF TOTAL REPLACEMENT VALUE OF PLANT

PUBLIC

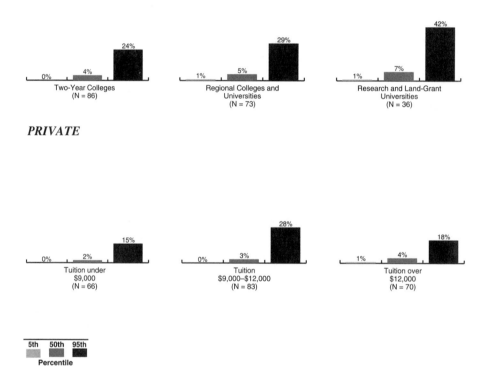

PRIVATE

5th   50th   95th
Percentile

QUESTIONS FOR POLICY MAKERS TO ASK

1. Has our institution done a systematic study of deferred maintenance?

2. What is the amount of our maintenance backlog? Has it increased or decreased in recent years?

3. Do we have a plan for reducing the backlog? Where will the funding come from?

4. How can we ensure that future plant funding adequately provides for long-term maintenance, renewal, and replacement?

New investment in plant as a percent of plant depreciation at replacement value
New investment in plant as a percent of plant depreciation at book value

SIGNIFICANCE

Annual plant depreciation is a measure of the degree to which the value of plant is "used up" or depleted during the year. The measure is based on an estimate of the useful life of each building. For example, if a building's useful life were estimated to be 20 years, annual depreciation would be one-twentieth of either the book or replacement value of that building. Book value is the original cost of the building, while replacement value is the estimated cost of constructing it today. Clearly, replacement value is a more meaningful measure, since it takes into account the effects of inflation. However, book value is the more common measure because it is static and therefore does not require annual reassessment.

Comparing new investment in plant with plant depreciation provides an estimate of the degree to which an institution is replacing depleted plant. Ideally, new investment should equal or exceed depreciation, since the failure to do so means that eventually the institution will use up all of its plant's value.

INTERPRETATION

As a percent of book value, all institution groups are more than covering plant depreciation with new investment, exceeding it by rates ranging from 12 percent in public research universities to 53 percent in public two-year colleges. However, a more troubling picture emerges when replacement value of plant is taken into account. Only among mid and high-tuition private institutions did new investment in plant exceed depreciation at replacement value. Low-tuition private colleges barely covered their depreciation with new investment, while public two-year and regional institutions lost ground to depreciation. Too few public research universities responding to the survey provided information about depreciation at replacement value to enable a figure to be reported here. And, among all institution groups, fewer reported depreciation at replacement value than at book value. This suggests that, while all institutions are aware of the book value of their plant, many fewer know its current value, which may be a cause for concern as plans for renovation and new construction are developed.

NEW INVESTMENT IN PLANT AS A PERCENT OF PLANT DEPRECIATION AT REPLACEMENT VALUE

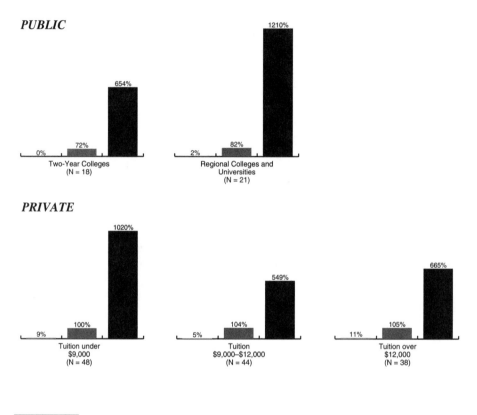

PUBLIC

1210%

654%

72%

0%

Two-Year Colleges
(N = 18)

82%

2%

Regional Colleges and
Universities
(N = 21)

PRIVATE

1020%

100%

9%

Tuition under
$9,000
(N = 48)

549%

104%

5%

Tuition
$9,000–$12,000
(N = 44)

665%

105%

11%

Tuition over
$12,000
(N = 38)

5th 50th 95th
Percentile

NEW INVESTMENT IN PLANT AS A PERCENT OF PLANT DEPRECIATION AT BOOK VALUE

PUBLIC

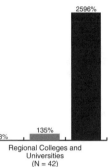

	2596%	
926%		1130%
2% 153%	3% 135%	7% 112%
Two-Year Colleges (N = 29)	Regional Colleges and Universities (N = 42)	Research and Land-Grant Universities (N = 12)

PRIVATE

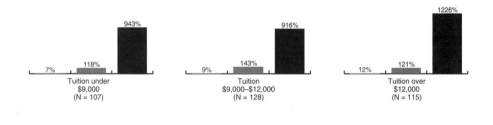

		1226%
943%	916%	
7% 118%	9% 143%	12% 121%
Tuition under $9,000 (N = 107)	Tuition $9,000–$12,000 (N = 128)	Tuition over $12,000 (N = 115)

5th	50th	95th

Percentile

QUESTIONS FOR POLICY MAKERS TO ASK

1. What percentage of our plant's depreciation is being covered by new investment, and how does that compare with our peers?

2. What have been recent trends in the ratio of new investment to plant depreciation?

3. Do we use book value, replacement value, or both to gauge the worth of our plant?

4. Does the institution fund plant depreciation? If not, what are our plans for financing needed replacement and renovation?

Information Capital

Book and monograph volumes per FTE student

SIGNIFICANCE

Library and other information resources represent an ongoing investment in knowledge. Given the accelerating "knowledge explosion," adequate library resources are essential to learning and research. When finances are strained, many institutions curtail library budgets and new acquisitions, as well as reduce expenditures for journal subscriptions and other learning resources. Over time, collections may become dated, and their value to students and faculty diminished.

In addition to monitoring volumes per FTE student, policy makers can study trends in their institution's acquisition of new volumes. For libraries which regularly cull outdated materials from their collections and replace them with new books, volumes per FTE student may remain static, even while the collection is being revitalized.

Many institutions are obtaining more materials through interlibrary loan, consortial arrangements, and computer networks in order to preserve scarce book-buying funds. Therefore, policy makers should evaluate the size of their library collections in light of the accessibility to students and faculty of other learning resources.

INTERPRETATION

The size of library collections on a per-student basis varies directly with institutional wealth, selectivity, and prestige. That is, within the private sector, the lowest tuition colleges have the smallest library collections per student, followed by the mid-tuition institutions, and then by the high-tuition colleges. In the public sector, research university collections are more than three times the size of two-year college libraries, on a per-student basis, with regional institutions falling between these two extremes.

BOOK AND MONOGRAPH VOLUMES PER FTE STUDENT

PUBLIC

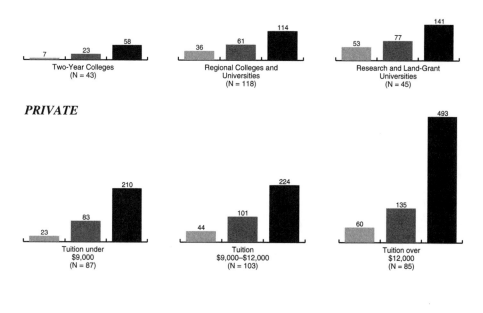

PRIVATE

QUESTIONS FOR POLICY MAKERS TO ASK

1. What is the size of our library collection, and how does it compare with peers?

2. What have been recent trends in the size of the collection?

3. Can we quickly, easily, and inexpensively arrange to obtain materials not in our collection when we need them?

4. Is technology changing our posture about the investment we should make in books and monographs?

5. How have library acquisition budgets been faring in recent years?

Internet access

Percent of institutions that provide full Internet access
Percent of institutions with networks that provide partial Internet access
Percent of institutions that provide no Internet access
Percent of institutions with Internet connections that provide access to:
   E-mail
   Gopher
   FTP
   Telnet
   News lists
   List serves

SIGNIFICANCE

Growth of the Internet has been of major importance for higher education during the last few years. From its initial objective of providing faculty researchers access to remote mainframe computers, the "net" has become an information superhighway available to virtually anyone. Faculty and student users can communicate with one another freely via electronic mail, regardless of distance. They can access library catalogues around the world and increasingly obtain full-text documents from authors, publishers, and archives. A world of information is available from government and corporate servers, as well as from colleges, universities, and other nonprofit entities. Increasingly, faculty are expecting students to make use of these resources, not only for independent research, but also in connection with course assignments.

Mere access to the Internet no longer puts an institution in the fast lane of the information superhighway. The connection must be fast enough to allow multiple users to download extensive files and graphics without undue delay. (The World-Wide Web, with its rich array of graphics, makes particularly heavy demands on bandwidth.) Modern configurations also support a broad array of services in addition to electronic mail. These include access to the Web and its text-oriented predecessor (the Gopher), the ability to transfer files (FTP) and run remote computers (Telnet), and special information sources such as news lists and list services.

INTERPRETATION

Internet access is greatest among public research universities—100 percent or nearly so on every measure—followed closely by regional public institutions. Among private institutions, access generally varies according to tuition level, with the greatest access found at the mid- and high-tuition institutions. Access is lowest among public two-year colleges and low-tuition private institutions. Nevertheless, even among these institutions, approximately 80 to 90 percent offer full or partial access to the Internet, and, among those, a considerable majority provide access to a wide range of Internet-related services.

INTERNET ACCESS

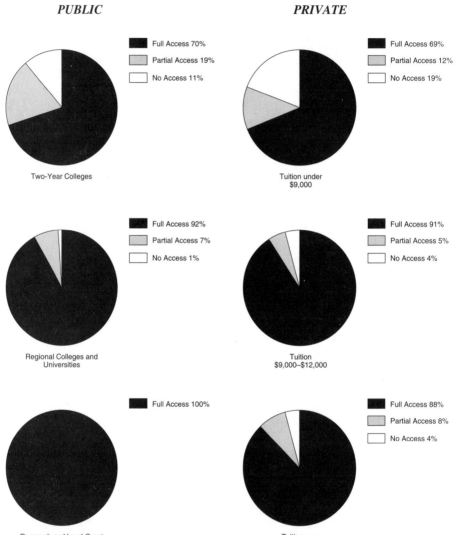

PUBLIC

Full Access 70%
Partial Access 19%
No Access 11%

Two-Year Colleges

Full Access 92%
Partial Access 7%
No Access 1%

Regional Colleges and
Universities

Full Access 100%

Research and Land-Grant
Universities

PRIVATE

Full Access 69%
Partial Access 12%
No Access 19%

Tuition under
$9,000

Full Access 91%
Partial Access 5%
No Access 4%

Tuition
$9,000–$12,000

Full Access 88%
Partial Access 8%
No Access 4%

Tuition over
$12,000

ACCESS TO INTERNET SERVICES

	Public Two-year	Public Regional Colleges and Universities	Public Research and Land-Grant Universities	Private tuition under $9,000	Private tuition $9,000–$12,000	Private tuition over $12,000
E-Mail	97%	99%	100%	95%	100%	98%
Gopher	87%	98%	100%	79%	94%	92%
FTP	87%	96%	100%	91%	96%	94%
Telnet	88%	98%	100%	91%	96%	94%
News Lists	65%	84%	98%	51%	55%	72%
List Serves	80%	92%	98%	72%	80%	89%

A note about this table: The percentages shown here all refer to the subset of institutions reporting full or partial access to the Internet.

QUESTIONS FOR POLICY MAKERS TO ASK

1. Does our institution have a direct connection to the Internet?

2. Does the connection have sufficient speed (bandwidth) to accommodate peak-hour usage without serious response-time degradation?

3. Does the network configuration support the whole array or Internet services, or is it limited to e-mail and related services?

4. How is the Internet used to support teaching, research, and public service at the institution?

5. Do we have any plans to upgrade access our to the Internet?

On-campus connectivity

Percent of respondents with central wide-band computer networks
        fiber optic central spine
        coaxial cable central spine
        other central spine
Percent of administrative offices with connections to the network
Percent of faculty/staff offices with connections to the network
Percent of libraries with connections to the network
Percent with library catalogue on the network
Percent of classrooms/labs with connections to the network
Percent of student residence hall rooms with connections to the network

SIGNIFICANCE

Connectivity has become the new litmus test of an institution's information technology capacity. Computers cannot perform effectively without communicating with servers and databases and with the Internet. A school cannot reap the benefits of information technology without an effective on-campus network that reaches most, if not all, campus computers and without full access to the Internet.

By connecting administrative offices to the network, an institution can provide electronic mail services and position itself to take advantage of on-line transaction processing and integrated information systems. Given proper software, for example, networked administrators can input financial, procurement, and personnel transactions on line for central processing and then download information from central files for local analysis and action. Investments in connectivity are necessary preconditions for the economies and improved performance associated with the paperless office.

Connecting faculty computers to the central network can improve academic productivity by providing electronic mail and on-line access to library resources, databases, and teaching materials. Student connectivity is becoming more important for the same reasons, and it also aids interaction with faculty through electronic mail, as well as the ability to run simulations and other class-based exercises and to receive and send class assignments electronically.

To claim status as an electronic campus, an institution should offer 100 percent network access to both students and faculty.

INTERPRETATION

Approximately 80 percent of all institutions responding to the survey have central wide-band computer networks. Within each sector, the percentage of institutions with networks rises with institutional wealth, prestige, and selectivity. That is, it is highest in public research universities and high-tuition private colleges and lowest in two-year public and low-tuition private institutions.

The vast majority of institutions in all groups report having fiber-optic central spines.

Of those institutions with central wide-band networks, the highest proportions of connections are to libraries, and, again, research universities and high-tuition private colleges are those most likely to have connected libraries. The same pattern holds for library catalogues and student residence hall rooms.

Overall, libraries and offices are far more likely to be connected to the network than classrooms and student residence hall rooms.

RESPONDENTS WITH CENTRAL WIDE-BAND COMPUTER NETWORKS

	Public Two-year	Public Regional Colleges and Universities	Public Research and Land-Grant Universities	Private tuition under $9,000	Private tuition $9,000– $12,000	Private tuition over $12,000
Campus-wide network	73%	94%	93%	67%	75%	92%
Central spine of the network is:						
Fiber optic	73%	89%	90%	71%	76%	85%
Coaxial cable	16%	7%	5%	16%	14%	6%
Other	11%	4%	5%	13%	10%	9%

CONNECTIVITY OF CAMPUS FACILITIES TO THE NETWORK*

	Public Two-year	Public Regional Colleges and Universities	Public Research and Land-Grant Universities	Private tuition under $9,000	Private tuition $9,000–$12,000	Private tuition over $12,000
Connections to the network:						
Administrative offices	89%	91%	86%	87%	82%	88%
Faculty/staff offices	69%	83%	73%	72%	75%	83%
Libraries	90%	95%	100%	84%	91%	93%
Library catalogs	63%	87%	93%	64%	71%	87%
Classrooms/labs	42%	51%	32%	47%	52%	52%
Student residence rooms	11%	19%	23%	25%	32%	43%

*A note about this table: The percentages shown here refer to the subset of institutions reporting the presence of a central wide-band computer network on campus.

QUESTIONS FOR POLICY MAKERS TO ASK

1. Does our institution have a central wide-bandwidth on-campus data network ("spine")?

2. What proportion of academic, administrative, and residence buildings are wired into the network, and how do we compare with peers?

3. What proportion of all faculty and administrative offices, classrooms and labs, and student residences hall rooms are wired into the network, and how do we compare with peers?

4. Do we have plans to increase connectivity on the campus?

Student access to computers

FTE students per microcomputer supplied for student use
**Percent of institutions that require full-time students
to have computers**
**Percent of institutions that require part-time students to
have computers**
**Percent of institutions with a formal policy for funding
depreciation of computer equipment**

SIGNIFICANCE

Internet access and on-campus connectivity will have little impact on education if students cannot access the workstations needed to take advantage of these resources. Moreover, modern educational practice relied on student access to microcomputers to access multimedia programs, process data, and run simulations in addition to word processing and obtaining information and communicating by e-mail in connection with courses. To take full advantage of information technology's potential to leverage learning, institutions need to ensure that all students can access a microcomputer as easily as previous generations accessed typewriters and electronic calculators.

Most institutions initially provided students with computer access through central "computer halls"—rooms filled with microcomputers where students could go to do their assignments. The typical next move was to disperse these resources to more convenient locations such as departments, residence halls, and in come cases even to individual student rooms. Whether microcomputers are central or dispersed, institutions must recognize that computer expenditures must be budgeted on an annual basis. This is usually done by funding annual depreciation of the computer stock, with a depreciation period as short as three or four years.

Requiring students to acquire their own computers represents an nascent trend. Sometimes the acquisition is facilitated by the institution through general tuition or special fees in order to ensure standardization. Whether institutionally facilitated or not, student ownership offers the advantage of ubiquitous access plus an opportunity for students and faculty to make the computer a natural and indispensable part of the learning process.

INTERPRETATION

On average, institutions supply approximately one microcomputer for every 15 full-time-equivalent students. While the lowest numbers of students per computer are seen at two-year public and high-tuition private colleges, there is considerable consistency among institutions on this measure, ranging from 10 to 19.

Very few institutions require even their full-time students to own computers, especially in the public sector. The high-tuition private institution group is most likely to make this a requirement, but nevertheless, only three percent of institutions do so. For part-time students, virtually no institutions require ownership of computers.

Perhaps because the government appropriations process does not allow many public institutions to make long-term financial plans, few public institutions have a formal policy for funding depreciation of computer equipment. By contrast, more than one-quarter of all private institutions have such policies in place.

FTE STUDENTS PER MICROCOMPUTER SUPPLIED FOR STUDENT USE

PUBLIC

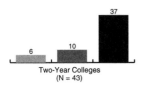

Two-Year Colleges
(N = 43)

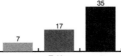

Regional Colleges and
Universities
(N = 116)

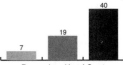

Research and Land-Grant
Universities
(N = 41)

PRIVATE

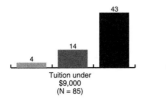

Tuition under
$9,000
(N = 85)

Tuition
$9,000–$12,000
(N = 100)

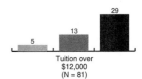

Tuition over
$12,000
(N = 81)

5th 50th 95th
Percentile

COMPUTER REQUIREMENTS AND POLICIES

Source	Public Two-year	Public Regional Colleges and Universities	Public Research and Land-Grant Universities	Private tuition under $9,000	Private tuition $9,000– $12,000	Private tuition over $12,000
Full-time undergrads required to have a computer	1%	0	0	2%	1%	3%
Part-time undergrads required to have a computer	1%	0	0	0	0	0
Percent of institutions with a formal depreciation policy	7%	10%	3%	29%	28%	27%

QUESTIONS FOR POLICY MAKERS TO ASK

1. Are there sufficient numbers of microcomputers on campus to meet student demand? How do we compare with our peers on this measure?

2. Are students satisfied with microcomputer capabilities? Are microcomputers adequately supported?

3. Is the institution making adequate investments in academic computing and other learning technology? Do we depreciate our investments (and fund the depreciation) to ensure regular replacement and upgrades?

4. Has the institution considered the possibility of asking students to acquire their own computers, perhaps with institutional facilitation?

Percent of institutions with a chief information officer

SIGNIFICANCE

An institution's information capital represents one of its most important strategic assets. Historically, library resources represented the bulk of information capital, and librarians were the key managers of this resource. Now, however, the library represents only a portion of information capital, and even it is being transformed by digital information technology.

Increasing numbers of institutions are recognizing the need to integrate the planning and implementation of information resources and are appointing a chief information officer to lead this effort. This person is generally expected to have a strong command of modern information technology and be able to organize complex projects as well as understand academe and the contributions of information technology to teaching and learning, scholarship, and administration.

INTERPRETATION

On average, approximately one-quarter of all institutions responding to the survey have a chief information officer. Percentages are generally higher in the public sector, particularly among regional colleges and universities, where one-third reported having an individual assigned to this function.

PERCENT OF INSTITUTIONS WITH A
CHIEF INFORMATION OFFICER

Public Two-year	Public Regional Colleges and Universities	Public Research and Land-Grant Universities	Private tuition under $9,000	Private tuition $9,000–$12,000	Private tuition over $12,000
27%	34%	25%	29%	22%	19%

QUESTIONS FOR POLICY MAKERS TO ASK

1. Does our institution have a chief information officer?

2. If so, does he or she have responsibility for coordinating all information resources, including networking, student computer access, administrative computing, and library resources?

3. If we do not currently have such a position, how are our information resources coordinated? Should we consider designating a chief information officer?

Human Capital

Fall 1994 total FTE students as a percent of Fall 1993 total FTE students

SIGNIFICANCE

Enrollment is the lifeblood of most institutions, which exist primarily to educate students. Change in enrollment from one year to the next is virtually always monitored very closely, particularly by less selective institutions, which, by definition, are more affected by the vicissitudes of student applications, yield, and rates of retention.

Enrollment changes can reflect student or institutional choices or a combination of the two. They may signify an increase or decrease in demand by students or potential students caused by factors such as changes in the local population of college-aged students or the success of admissions marketing efforts; inability, especially in the private sector, to meet the financial-aid needs of potential students; a conscious effort by the institution to restrict or increase enrollment by altering admission standards; or an alteration in the proportion of full-time to part-time students.

The financial impact of enrollment decreases depends to a great extent on an institution's tuition dependence. For example, a college with a large endowment and strong fund-raising performance, or one with public appropriations not directly tied to enrollment, can weather a loss of students better than one for which tuition income is its sole key revenue source or for which public appropriations drop in proportion to enrollment decline. The financial impact of enrollment increases depends on factors such as demand by additional students for institutional financial aid, access to supplemental public appropriations, and the availability of excess physical plant capacity to accommodate additional students.

INTERPRETATION

Survey data show slight increases in enrollment among all private institution groups and stability or slight decreases among all public sector cohorts. Enrollment declined most in the two-year public institutions, which, for many years, have been under enormous pressure to absorb additional students. They may simply have been pushed past their limit and now are trying to reach a lower enrollment they can more easily accommodate. In addition, unemployment is near historic lows, and there may be slightly less demand for enrollment in community colleges, which historically have attracted, among others, individuals seeking job training and re-training. Overall, these data reflect stable demand for higher education, despite declines in the population of traditional college-aged students.

FALL 1994 TOTAL FTE STUDENTS AS A PERCENT OF FALL 1993 TOTAL FTE STUDENTS

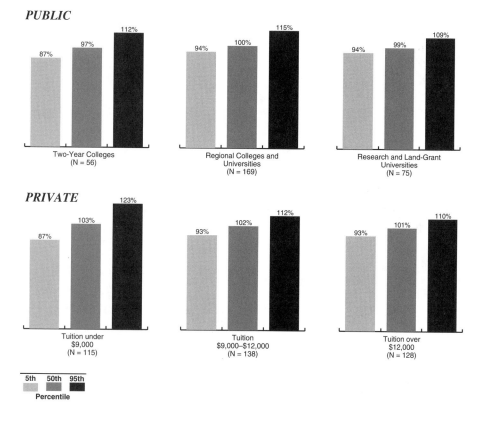

QUESTIONS FOR POLICY MAKERS TO ASK

1. What have been the recent trends in enrollment at our institution?
2. What accounts for any changes we have witnessed?

3. How do these changes affect other aspects of our institution, such as the health of our overall budget picture, demand for classes, use of physical plant, and morale of the campus?

4. What steps is our college or university taking to manage the enrollment picture and its effects on the institution?

Percent of total FTE students who are part-time

SIGNIFICANCE

The population of traditional college-aged students has declined in recent years, and currently the fastest growing segment of the American population is the 35 years and older cohort. As a result, many colleges and universities have moved aggressively into the market for part-time students, most of whom are working adults.

Part-time students affect an institution in a variety of ways. Often, they need services tailored to non-resident adults who may have been away from formal education for some time. These students may be more interested in career-oriented programs than their younger, full-time counterparts, and they may alter demand for many of the institution's facilities and services. For example, because it takes several part-time students to equal one full-time student, services such as libraries and student advising facilities may be overtaxed. At the same time, demand for residence halls and traditional student activities may decline as part-time enrollment increases.

INTERPRETATION

Two-year public colleges enroll far more part-time students than any other institutional segment. This is a predictable finding, given the historic mission of community colleges to serve the needs of working adults. The proportion of students enrolled part-time is lowest, among private institutions, in the high-tuition group and, among public institutions, in research universities. Because these are the most selective institutions, survey results suggest that pursuit of the part-time student market is a reaction to decreasing demand for full-time enrollment in less selective institutions.

PERCENT OF TOTAL FTE STUDENTS WHO ARE PART-TIME

PUBLIC

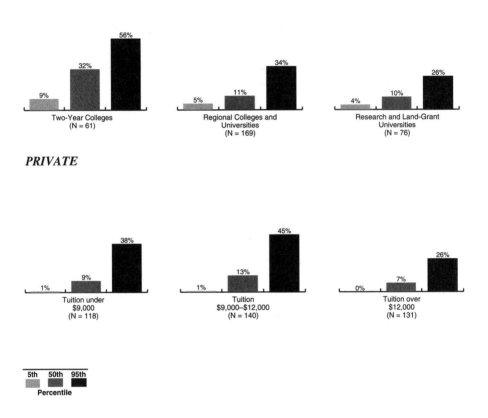

PRIVATE

QUESTIONS FOR POLICY MAKERS TO ASK

1. What have been the recent trends in part-time enrollment at our institution, and how does our enrollment of part-time students compare with our peers?

2. Have changes in part-time enrollment resulted from a conscious institutional strategy?

3. What effects have changes in part-time enrollments had on use of our facilities and services?

4. Have we altered our program offerings and support services in response to the differing needs and interests of part-time students?

FTE enrollment by racial/ethnic status
Hispanic FTE students as a percent of total FTE students
Asian and Pacific Islander FTE students as a percent of total FTE students
Black FTE students as a percent of total FTE students

SIGNIFICANCE

The racial and ethnic composition of the American population is changing rapidly, and many colleges and universities are trying to diversify their student bodies. Public discussion and controversy surrounding affirmative action programs may affect institutions' ability to attract the diverse student bodies many say they desire. This is particularly the case in public institutions, which are subject to state laws permitting or curtailing affirmative action.

In general, enrollment by racial/ethnic status may reflect the success of affirmative action programs, the institution's geographical location, availability of financial aid, the historical and current mission of the institution, and a campus's openness to diversity.

INTERPRETATION

Minority students are more likely to be enrolled in public sector institutions and, within that sector, are more apt to be enrolled in two-year colleges. Within the private sector, enrollment of black students drops as tuition charges rise, but enrollment of Asian/Pacific Islander and, to some extent, Hispanic students increases with rises in tuition charges. Nevertheless, black students represent overall a significantly higher proportion of college and university enrollments than Asian/Pacific Islander, Hispanic, and Native American students combined.

Native American students represent well under one percent of enrollments in all institutional categories and thus are not reported here.

FTE ENROLLMENT BY RACIAL/ETHNIC STATUS

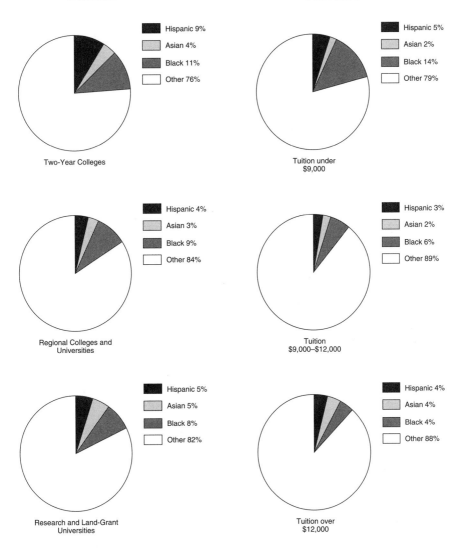

PUBLIC

Two-Year Colleges

Hispanic 9%
Asian 4%
Black 11%
Other 76%

Regional Colleges and
Universities

Hispanic 4%
Asian 3%
Black 9%
Other 84%

Research and Land-Grant
Universities

Hispanic 5%
Asian 5%
Black 8%
Other 82%

PRIVATE

Tuition under
$9,000

Hispanic 5%
Asian 2%
Black 14%
Other 79%

Tuition
$9,000–$12,000

Hispanic 3%
Asian 2%
Black 6%
Other 89%

Tuition over
$12,000

Hispanic 4%
Asian 4%
Black 4%
Other 88%

QUESTIONS FOR POLICY MAKERS TO ASK

1. What have been the recent trends in enrollment by racial/ethnic status at our institution, and how does our enrollment of minority students compare with our peers?

2. Do these trends reflect conscious institutional efforts, and are we satisfied with these efforts?

3. Do our minority student populations differ systematically from one another and from the majority population in terms of academic preparedness, academic interests, retention, satisfaction with the institution, or other factors?

4. What efforts is the institution making to improve the campus climate for minority students?

Female FTE students as a percent of total FTE students

SIGNIFICANCE

The number of women in the general population is slightly higher than that of men, a trend that also is evident in the student body of many colleges and universities. Enrollment of women also may be greater because many women are marrying later and entering the work force in larger numbers, making higher education an attractive option.

Enrollment by women in higher education has been an important factor in overall enrollment increases for the past several years. Projections by the U.S. Department of Education indicate that enrollment by women in higher education will continue to surpass enrollment by men. However, at some institutions, there may be a conscious effort to manage the ratio of men to women in the student body. Also, a small number of institutions are single-sex, admitting only men or only women.

INTERPRETATION

Survey data indicate that women are a majority of total FTE students in all institutional categories. Within the public group, public research universities enroll the smallest percentage of women, at 51 percent, while high-tuition colleges enroll the smallest percentage of women—54 percent—seen in the private group. All other institutional categories are remarkably consistent, at 56 to 57 percent women.

FEMALE FTE STUDENTS AS A PERCENT OF TOTAL FTE STUDENTS

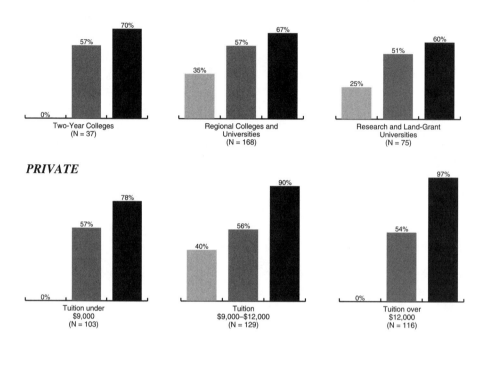

PUBLIC

Two-Year Colleges
(N = 37)
0% — 57% — 70%

Regional Colleges and Universities
(N = 168)
35% — 57% — 67%

Research and Land-Grant Universities
(N = 75)
25% — 51% — 60%

PRIVATE

Tuition under $9,000
(N = 103)
0% — 57% — 78%

Tuition $9,000–$12,000
(N = 129)
40% — 56% — 90%

Tuition over $12,000
(N = 116)
0% — 54% — 97%

5th   50th   95th
Percentile

QUESTIONS FOR POLICY MAKERS TO ASK

1. What have been the recent trends in enrollment by women and men at our institution, and how does our enrollment of women and men compare with our peers?

2. Do these trends reflect conscious institutional policy or are they coincidental?

3. Do our women students differ systematically from the male student population in terms of academic preparedness, academic interests, retention, satisfaction with the institution, or other factors?

4. Are any changes needed to improve the campus climate (e.g., campus safety) for female or male students?

Percent of total students from outside the U.S. and Canada

SIGNIFICANCE

American higher education is considered the envy of the world in quality, breadth, and access, and increasingly colleges and universities in this country are attracting students from other nations. Foreign students can shore up enrollments, enhance the diversity of the student body, and preserve institutional financial aid dollars, since these students often pay full tuition. At the same time, they can absorb significant resources for language instruction and special counseling and advising.

Factors that can influence enrollment by foreign students include the extent to which the institution is known internationally, along with the distinctiveness or perceived quality of its programs and their pertinence to the needs of the home country. Enrollment also may be affected by financial issues such as the changing value of foreign currencies relative to the dollar and, for public institutions, policies that result in especially high or low tuition and fees charged to foreign students. In addition, some public institutions may limit enrollment by foreign students in order to reserve more places for citizens of the state.

INTERPRETATION

Survey data indicate that the percent of foreign students tends to increase with institutional cost, prestige, and selectivity (which also tends to be correlated with institutional visibility and perceived quality). Foreign enrollments are lowest among public two-year colleges, slightly higher among regional institutions, and higher yet within the research universities. Within the private sector, the percentage of students from foreign nations is lowest among the low-tuition group and greatest within the mid- and high-tuition categories.

PERCENT OF TOTAL STUDENTS FROM OUTSIDE THE U.S. AND CANADA

PUBLIC

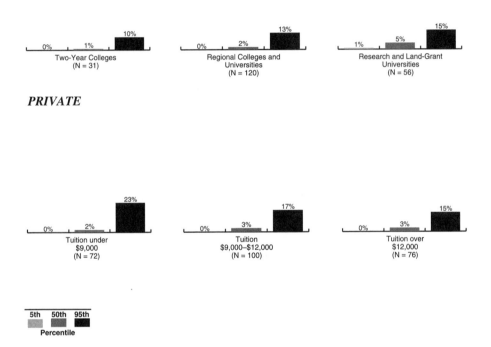

PRIVATE

5th 50th 95th
Percentile

QUESTIONS FOR POLICY MAKERS TO ASK

1. What proportion of our institution's student body comes from other countries, how does this compare with peers, and does this number represent a significant percentage of our student body?

2. How satisfied are our foreign students with their experience at this institution?

3. If we would like to increase enrollment of foreign students, do we offer programs they would find attractive? Would we need to add special services to meet their needs? At what cost?

4. How might we go about attracting additional foreign students, if that is our goal?

Percent of total students from within the state

SIGNIFICANCE

Many institutions, especially in the private sector, seek national student bodies because geographic diversity is associated with selectivity and prestige. Moreover, these institutions claim that the educational experience itself is enhanced by having students from across the country (and around the world) studying together. Geographic diversity has other, practical, advantages as well. A college or university that is able to attract a national student body will far less affected by local demographic and economic trends, which may be in decline.

An institution's ability to attract students from other states depends on the reach of its reputation, the distinctiveness of its programs, and its aggressiveness in recruiting broadly. For public institutions, enrollment by out-of-state students can be affected by policies that limit enrollment by non-state residents or that charge especially high or low tuition and fees to these students.

INTERPRETATION

In general, in-state enrollment declines as institutional selectivity and prestige increase, though more than half of all students enrolled in all categories of institutions are from within the state. The highest level of in-state enrollment—98 percent—is seen at two-year public colleges, virtually all of whose enrollments are local. The lowest levels of in-state enrollments—averaging 58 percent—are found in high-tuition private institutions.

PERCENT OF TOTAL STUDENTS FROM WITHIN THE STATE

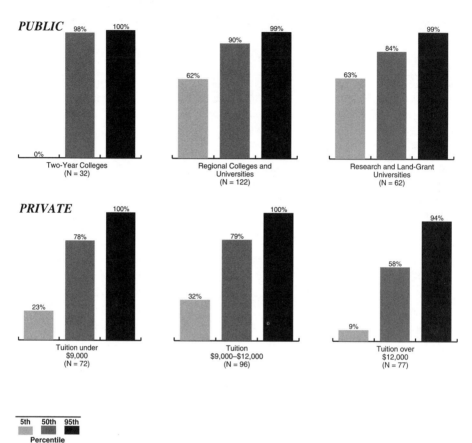

PUBLIC

Two-Year Colleges
(N = 32)
98% 100%

Regional Colleges and
Universities
(N = 122)
62% 90% 99%

Research and Land-Grant
Universities
(N = 62)
63% 84% 99%

PRIVATE

Tuition under
$9,000
(N = 72)
23% 78% 100%

Tuition
$9,000–$12,000
(N = 96)
32% 79% 100%

Tuition over
$12,000
(N = 77)
9% 58% 94%

5th 50th 95th
Percentile

QUESTIONS FOR POLICY MAKERS TO ASK

1. What proportion of our institution's student body comes from within the state, and how does this compare with peers?

2. If we would like to increase enrollment of out-of-state students, how might we go about attracting them?

Percent of freshman applicants accepted
Percent of transfer applicants accepted

SIGNIFICANCE

The proportions of freshman and transfer applicants accepted are fundamental indicators of institutional selectivity. Rates of acceptance are influenced by a wide range of factors, internal and extrinsic to the institution. Institutions have mission statements, strategies, and admission standards that define the number and kinds of students who are acceptable. Demand for programs the institution offers may rise or fall, and, in the public sector, acceptance rates can be affected by enrollment caps resulting from decreased appropriations. Retention rates of upper class students affect the number of "slots" available to new students. And residential and other space on campus may be overtaxed or, alternatively, have excess capacity.

The availability of non-tuition revenues can give institutions greater flexibility in dealing with growth or diminution in student applications. These revenues can cushion the effects of enrollment declines, provide financial aid to make enrollment affordable to more students, or enable an institution to hire more faculty and staff or add to the physical plant.

An institution may relax its admission standards in order to attract sufficient numbers of students, though in doing so the college's reputation may suffer. It may also find it must offer more remedial courses, tutoring, and advising, all of which can drive up institutional costs.

INTERPRETATION

Public research universities are more selective than the regional institution group, and the average two-year college is an open-admissions institution. Among private colleges, selectivity is highest in the high-tuition group. These observations reinforce the conclusion that tuition levels are linked to institutional desirability, status, and/or real or perceived quality.

Among public institutions (except for two-year colleges), selectivity is higher for freshmen than for transfers, perhaps because more public-sector students begin in community colleges or branch institutions and transfer to upper division universities. The opposite pattern is seen in the private sector, where selectivity is higher for transfer students than for freshmen.

PERCENT OF FRESHMAN APPLICANTS ACCEPTED

PUBLIC

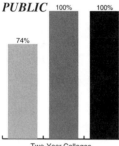

Two-Year Colleges
(N = 169)

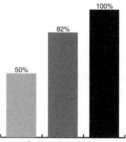

Regional Colleges and
Universities
(N = 157)

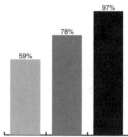

Research and Land-Grant
Universities
(N = 71)

PRIVATE

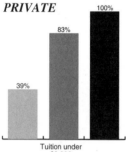

Tuition under
$9,000
(N = 132)

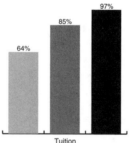

Tuition
$9,000–$12,000
(N = 159)

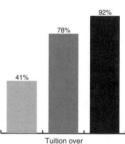

Tuition over
$12,000
(N = 154)

5th	50th	95th

Percentile

PERCENT OF TRANSFER APPLICANTS ACCEPTED

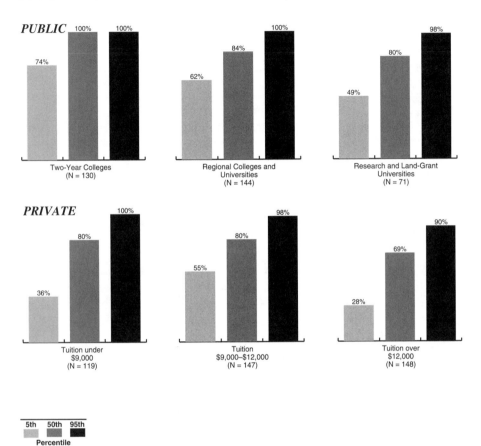

PUBLIC

Two-Year Colleges (N = 130): 74%, 100%, 100%

Regional Colleges and Universities (N = 144): 62%, 84%, 100%

Research and Land-Grant Universities (N = 71): 49%, 80%, 98%

PRIVATE

Tuition under $9,000 (N = 119): 36%, 80%, 100%

Tuition $9,000–$12,000 (N = 147): 55%, 80%, 98%

Tuition over $12,000 (N = 148): 28%, 69%, 90%

5th   50th   95th
Percentile

QUESTIONS FOR POLICY MAKERS TO ASK

1. What have been recent trends in selectivity at our institution, and how do we compare with peers?

2. What accounts for any changes we have experienced?

3. What would be the long-term consequences of a continuation in our recent trends in selectivity?

4. Should we and can we make changes in our policies or institutional practices to increase or decrease our selectivity?

Percent of accepted freshmen who matriculate
Percent of accepted transfers who matriculate

SIGNIFICANCE

Admissions yield is the proportion of accepted applicants who matriculate. Yield is a function of a variety of competitive factors that influence potential students' choices among institutions. These include the relative attractiveness of the institution compared with competitors in terms of program offerings, location, campus facilities, and extracurricular offerings; the number of other institutions to which applicants apply and are accepted; and the total net costs of attending, taking into account the availability of financial aid.

Many students are applying to a larger number of institutions than used to be customary, resulting in decreased yield in a greater number of institutions. Especially in the private sector, students' decisions about where to enroll are being affected more than ever by the size of proffered financial aid packages, and institutional officials cite "bidding wars" for students who play one institution's financial aid offer off against another's.

INTERPRETATION

Accepted freshmen are less likely to matriculate as institutional selectivity rises, whether in the public or private sector. That is, among public institutions, matriculation rates are lowest among research institutions and highest in the community colleges. Within the private sector, matriculation rates decline as level of tuition (which is highly correlated with selectivity) rises. The pattern for transfer students is similar, though the transfer yield rates for public regional and research universities are virtually identical. These findings may suggest that students accepted by selective institutions apply to and are accepted by a greater number of schools. It also may suggest in the private sector that, as tuition rises, relatively fewer prospective students can afford to enroll.

PERCENT OF ACCEPTED FRESHMEN WHO MATRICULATE

PUBLIC

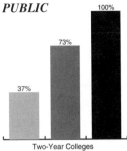

Two-Year Colleges
(N = 159)

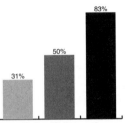

Regional Colleges and
Universities
(N = 158)

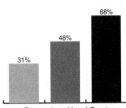

Research and Land-Grant
Universities
(N = 72)

PRIVATE

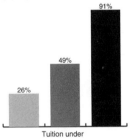

Tuition under
$9,000
(N = 134)

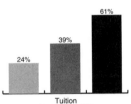

Tuition
$9,000–$12,000
(N = 158)

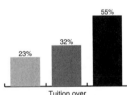

Tuition over
$12,000
(N = 152)

5th   50th   95th
Percentile

PERCENT OF ACCEPTED TRANSFERS WHO MATRICULATE

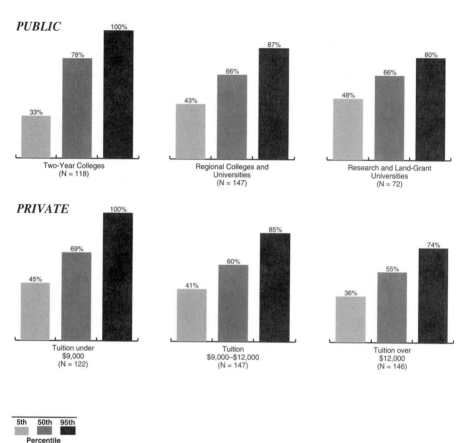

QUESTIONS FOR POLICY MAKERS TO ASK

1. What have been recent trends in matriculation rates at our institution, and how do they compare with peers?

2. What accounts for any changes we have experienced?

3. What would be the long-term consequences of a continuation in our recent matriculation trends?

4. Should we and can we make changes in our policies or institutional practices to increase our matriculation rates?

Degrees awarded
Associate degrees awarded as a percent of FTE enrollment
Baccalaureate degrees awarded as a percent of FTE enrollment
Master's degrees awarded as a percent of FTE enrollment

SIGNIFICANCE

Unless an institution intentionally enrolls many students who are not seeking degrees, the proportion of students who earn degrees is a measure of student progress and thus of institutional productivity.

Rates of degrees earned can be affected by many factors, including student choices. For example, part-time students necessarily take longer to earn degrees, while students who are able to attend full time, and who may have earned advanced placement credit while in high school, may finish relatively quickly.

The limits of institutional resources also may pay a role in rates of degrees earned. Much concern has been expressed recently, especially with respect to public colleges and universities, about delays in completing degrees because of institutions' inability to offer enough courses and sections to satisfy student demand. This circumstance is virtually unavoidable in situations where institutions are obliged to accept more students than they have resources to educate in a timely fashion.

In contrast to this situation, some colleges and universities are beginning to consider ways to improve "learner productivity" through altering educational requirements. The goal is to enable students to complete degrees in less time and at lower cost.

INTERPRETATION

Approximately 10 percent of the average public two-year college's FTE enrollment received associate degrees in 1995. This is a lower figure than the rate of baccalaureate degrees earned by students in four-year institutions, both public and private. Rates of baccalaureate degrees earned were higher in the private sector than the public and were highest of all—equivalent to 17 percent of FTE enrollment—in high-tuition private colleges, which, not coincidentally, also enroll the smallest number of part-time students.

Rates of master's degrees earned are much lower than baccalaureate completions, owing to lower enrollments in graduate programs. Rates of master's degree completions, in both the public and private sectors, rise with institutional prestige and selectivity. That is, in the public sector, they are higher in research universities than in regional institutions. In the private sector, they rise with tuition level. Quite possibly, all of the variance in master's degrees earned may be explained by relatively higher graduate enrollments in public research universities and higher-tuition private institutions.

We do not report median rates of first professional and doctoral degree achievement because only for the public research universities was the average response higher than zero. However, at the 95th percentile of responses, which would incorporate those institutions that award significant numbers of doctoral and first professional degrees, a pattern holds similar to that seen in completion of master's degrees. That is, completion rates rise with institutional selectivity and, in the private sector, level of tuition. As with master's degrees, the variance may be explained by the relatively higher enrollments in first professional and doctoral degree programs in research universities and higher-tuition private institutions.

ASSOCIATE DEGREES AWARDED AS A PERCENT OF FTE ENROLLMENT

PUBLIC

BACCALAUREATE DEGREES AWARDED AS A PERCENT OF FTE ENROLLMENT

PUBLIC

PRIVATE

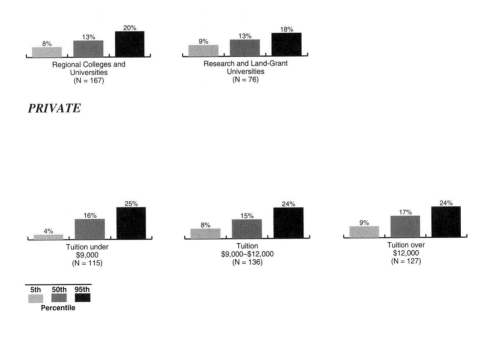

MASTER'S DEGREES AWARDED AS A PERCENT OF FTE ENROLLMENT

PUBLIC

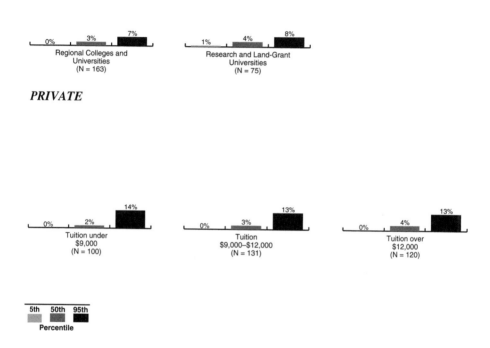

PRIVATE

5th   50th   95th
Percentile

QUESTIONS FOR POLICY MAKERS TO ASK

1. What have been recent trends in degrees earned at our institution, and how do they compare with peers?

2. What accounts for any changes we have experienced?

3. Are we satisfied with the rates at which our students are earning degrees?

4. Should we and can we make changes in our policies or institutional practices to increase our rate of degrees earned?

Institutional scholarship and fellowship expenditures as a percent of total tuition and fee income
Institutional scholarship and fellowship expenditures as a percent of total current fund expenditures

SIGNIFICANCE

Colleges and universities have tended to increase institutional financial aid in order to keep rising tuitions affordable for as many students as possible and to compete with the financial aid packages offered by peer institutions.

Institutions that devote a high percentage of their expenditures to finance student aid, or that return a high percentage of tuition and fees to students in the form of institutional financial aid, enhance their ability to attract students and achieve socioeconomic diversity, but often at the cost of diverting funds that otherwise could be available for academic programs. In other words, institutional financial aid reduces tuition revenue (i.e., it discounts tuition). Tuition discounting may be justified as long as net tuition (gross tuition revenue less institutionally funded financial aid) continues to grow and marginal income per student is greater than the marginal cost of educating that student.

This indicator should be viewed in conjunction with information about institutional selectivity. Less selective institutions that commit a large fraction of tuition to financial aid may be heading for financial difficulty, since their enrollment is directly dependent on offering tuition subsidies.

INTERPRETATION

Private colleges and universities, with their significantly higher tuition charges, provide a much larger tuition subsidy than public institutions do. As a percentage of total income from tuition and fees, institutional scholarships and fellowships average nearly 22 percent among all private institutions, compared with less than 6 percent among public colleges and universities.

A similar pattern holds when institutional scholarships and fellowships are viewed as a percentage of total current fund expenditures. Private institutions devote, on average, 13 percent of their current fund expenditures to institutionally funded scholarships and fellowships. The figure for public institutions is just over 1 percent.

In both the public and private sectors, expenditures of institutional funds for scholarships and fellowships increase, as a percentage of total expenditures and as a percentage of total tuition and fee income, as institutional costs and prestige rise.

INSTITUTIONAL SCHOLARSHIP AND FELLOWSHIP EXPENDITURES AS A PERCENT OF TOTAL TUITION AND FEE INCOME

PUBLIC

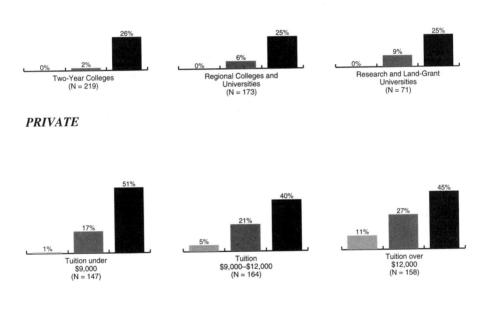

PRIVATE

INSTITUTIONAL SCHOLARSHIP AND FELLOWSHIP EXPENDITURES AS A PERCENT OF TOTAL CURRENT FUND EXPENDITURES

PUBLIC

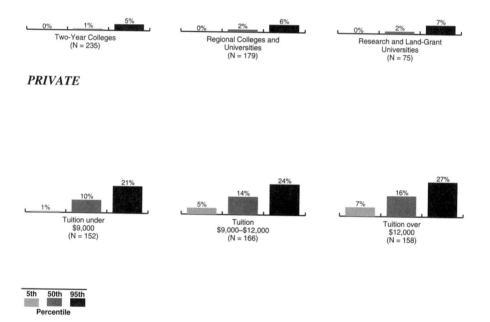

PRIVATE

QUESTIONS FOR POLICY MAKERS TO ASK

1. What have been the recent trends in tuition subsidies at our institution? What fraction of the incremental tuition dollar goes to financial aid?

2. What proportion of our tuition discounts come from unrestricted operating funds as opposed to such sources as endowment income or annual giving that are restricted to student aid?

3. What percentage of our students are "full pay," and what have been the trends in that figure?

4. What explains our trends in institutional financial aid, and what would be the consequences if they were to continue?

5. Is net tuition revenue growing?

Tuition and fees per undergraduate student (private)

SIGNIFICANCE

Tuition and fee charges in the private sector are a function of the institution's expenses, its dependence on tuition revenue as opposed to other sources such as private giving or endowment income, and the target student population's ability to pay. For most colleges and universities, tuition is the revenue source most under their direct control, and it tends to be used to fill the gap after other revenue sources have been exhausted.

The question of how prospective students and the public interpret tuition charges is controversial. Conventional wisdom used to hold that higher tuition was associated in the public mind with higher quality, and that, though students and their parents might grumble, they would pay the higher tuition in exchange for perceived higher quality and status. Moreover, as published tuitions have increased, many institutions, either by using endowment income or by shifting costs among students, have offered substantial tuition discounts, which have lessened for many students the real cost of attending these colleges and universities.

Perhaps because of discounting and resultant financial aid "bidding wars" among colleges and universities for prospective students, some observers believe that the public has become cynical about tuition charges and less willing to believe that a high published tuition rate equates to quality. Where previously parents would boast about the prestigious college that accepted their son or daughter, today's one-upmanship may be just as likely to concern the big "scholarship" the student received from a less prestigious college.

Whatever the explanation, which in part includes an easing of inflation, increases in private-sector tuition have moderated in recent years.

INTERPRETATION

The median charge for tuition and fees among all private institutions was just over $10,500 in fiscal year 1995.

TUITION AND FEES PER UNDERGRADUATE STUDENT (PRIVATE)

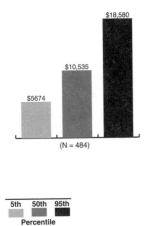

5th 50th 95th
Percentile

QUESTIONS FOR POLICY MAKERS TO ASK

1. Where do we stand with respect to the tuition and fee levels at peer institutions?

2. What have been the recent trends in rates of tuition and fee increases at our institution and in our position relative to peer institutions?

3. How have changes in tuition and fees co-varied with enrollment changes and tuition discounts? Does anything in this analysis suggest that tuition increases have been counterproductive?

4. What would be the consequences if tuition and fees were to increase at the current rate over the next few years?

Tuition and fees per in-state undergraduate student (public)
Tuition and fees per out-of-state undergraduate student (public)

SIGNIFICANCE

Tuition and fee charges in the public sector are a function of the institution's expenses, its dependence on tuition revenue as opposed to other sources such as appropriations or private giving, and the target student population's ability to pay. For most public colleges and universities, tuition is the revenue source most under their direct control, and it tends to be used to fill the gap after other revenue sources have been exhausted.

The ongoing public policy debate with respect to tuition concerns whether institutions should increase tuition charges and make more financial aid available to needy students, or whether instead public institutions should continue to keep tuition low for all, regardless of students' ability to pay. In part, opinions about this controversy are a function of how one views the purposes of public higher education. Is it largely a benefit to the individual, who should pay for it if financial circumstances allow? Or is it a public service like roads or fire protection, which should be available to all citizens under the same terms?

In a sense, circumstances seem to be overwhelming the argument. As states and localities have reduced the proportion of institutional budgets they finance, public institutions in many states have had little choice but to raise tuitions markedly, though in some cases availability of financial aid has not kept pace. In fact, it is not unusual for high need students to find that the actual cost of attending a private institution, after tuition discounts, is lower than the price charged by some public institutions.

Some public institutions, particularly those with high visibility and prestige, have been able to compensate partially for declines in appropriations by significantly increasing tuition charges to out-of-state students. However, some selective institutions argue that precipitous increases in out-of-state tuition can lead to a lessening of institutional diversity and overall student quality by discouraging the best out-of-state students from attending the institution. Also, many public institutions located near state borders rely on nearby out-of-state students to keep enrollment levels and overall tuition income high.

INTERPRETATION

In-state tuition among public institutions is lowest by far at two-year colleges, amounting to approximately 60 percent of that charged by regional and research institutions. On average, in-state tuition at public institutions is roughly 20 percent of the median tuition charged by private colleges and universities.

Out-of-state students at public institutions pay around three times the tuition and fees charged to in-state students, which amounts, on average, to about one-half of the tuition and fees charged by the average private institution.

TUITION AND FEES PER IN-STATE UNDERGRADUATE STUDENT (PUBLIC)

PUBLIC

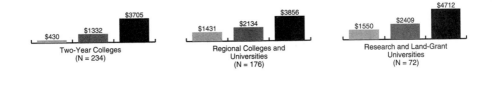

Two-Year Colleges (N = 234)	Regional Colleges and Universities (N = 176)	Research and Land-Grant Universities (N = 72)
$430 / $1332 / $3705	$1431 / $2134 / $3856	$1550 / $2409 / $4712

5th 50th 95th
Percentile

TUITION AND FEES PER OUT-OF-STATE UNDERGRADUATE STUDENT (PUBLIC)

PUBLIC

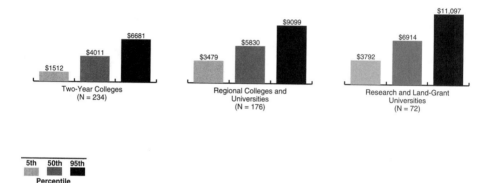

5th	50th	95th

Percentile

QUESTIONS FOR POLICY MAKERS TO ASK

1. What have been the recent trends in tuition and fees charged to out-of-state students?

2. How dependent is our institution on income from out-of-state students? Is this dependency growing or lessening?

3. Is there a quality differential between our in-state and out-of-state students? In other words, are we dependent on students from other states to shore up the average quality of our student body?

4. What evidence do we have that out-of-state students bring particular forms of diversity to our student body?

5. Is the political climate in our state or locality supportive or hostile to enrollment of out-of-state students?

Percent of students with institutional scholarships and fellowships

SIGNIFICANCE

Increasingly, colleges and universities are offering aid in the form of scholarships and fellowships in order to make tuition affordable to as many students as possible and to compete with the financial aid packages offered by peer institutions. Students who pay full tuition subsidize those who cannot afford the full price. As tuition rises, fewer students are able to pay full tuition, and more require subsidies, leading to spiraling need for institutional financial aid.

Institutions that can provide financial aid to a large proportion of their students may be better able to attract and retain those students, but they also may be committing resources to financial aid that could be used for other purposes, such as enhancing academic programs and facilities. Scholarships and fellowships that are financed with endowment or other income restricted to financial aid have less impact on the institution's financial position than those that are paid for with unrestricted current income.

INTERPRETATION

In the private sector, the proportion of students with institutional scholarship and fellowship aid is slightly higher at mid and high-tuition institutions than at low-tuition colleges. This may suggest that higher tuition institutions have more resources to devote to financial aid, that higher tuition makes relatively more students qualified for financial aid, or some combination of the two. In the public sector, a much smaller proportion of students receive institutional scholarship and fellowship aid, suggesting that more financial aid is received from external sources, that fewer students demonstrate need, and/or that there is less scholarship and fellowship aid available. As in the private sector, however, the proportion of students with scholarship and fellowship aid grows as institutional prestige (and cost) rise.

PERCENT OF STUDENTS WITH INSTITUTIONAL SCHOLARSHIPS AND FELLOWSHIPS

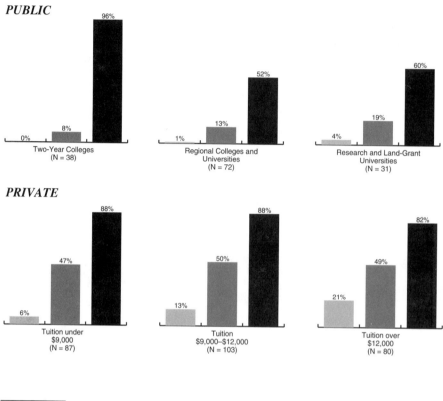

PUBLIC

Two-Year Colleges (N = 38): 0%, 8%, 96%

Regional Colleges and Universities (N = 72): 1%, 13%, 52%

Research and Land-Grant Universities (N = 31): 4%, 19%, 60%

PRIVATE

Tuition under $9,000 (N = 87): 6%, 47%, 88%

Tuition $9,000–$12,000 (N = 103): 13%, 50%, 88%

Tuition over $12,000 (N = 80): 21%, 49%, 82%

5th 50th 95th
Percentile

QUESTIONS FOR POLICY MAKERS TO ASK

1. What have been the recent trends in the percent of our students receiving institutional scholarship and fellowship aid?

2. What proportion of our scholarship and fellowship aid comes from unrestricted operating funds as opposed to such sources as endowment income or annual giving that are restricted to student aid?

3. What explains our trends in institutional scholarship and fellowship aid, and what would be the consequences if they were to continue?

Percent of students with institutional loans

SIGNIFICANCE

Rather than giving aid outright in the form of scholarships and fellowships, some colleges and universities make loans available to students from endowment or operating income. The value of such a program is that needy students receive the funds necessary to attend the institution, but, because the funds are paid back, the college can minimize the use of scarce operating funds for scholarship and fellowship aid. However, loan programs may put an institution at a competitive disadvantage with other schools that offer scholarships and fellowships rather than loans to a potential student, and these programs also can be expensive to administer. Moreover, excessive undergraduate loan burdens may discourage graduates from considering postgraduate education.

INTERPRETATION

Very few public or private institutions offer loans to their students, perhaps because, in a competitive market for students, scholarships and fellowships are far more attractive than loans. Moreover, loans are available from a variety of governmental and private sources, and students who wish to borrow money have options other than the institution.

PERCENT OF STUDENTS WITH INSTITUTIONAL LOANS

PUBLIC

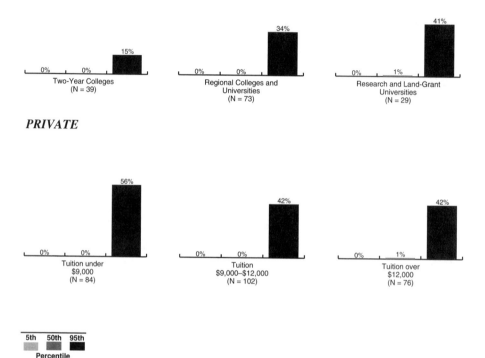

PRIVATE

5th   50th   95th
Percentile

QUESTIONS FOR POLICY MAKERS TO ASK

1. To what extent are institutional loans a factor in the financial aid packages our students receive, and what have been the recent trends?

2. What other sources of loans are available to our students, and what is the extent of the loan burden our students have undertaken?

3. Would an institutionally-sponsored loan program be an attractive way for our college or university to decrease our scholarship and fellowship burden? Would substituting loans for scholarships and fellowships put us at a disadvantage relative to competing institutions?

Percent of students with College Work-Study jobs

SIGNIFICANCE

The percentage of students who finance part of tuition and other costs through College Work-Study (CWS) employment is an indicator of the financial need of the student population relative to the costs of attending the institution. The more students who qualify for CWS and hold CWS jobs, the greater the relative need. A higher percentage of participation may also reflect the availability of CWS funds, an institution's success in creating positions and integrating students into the work force, and an institution's reliance on student employment to staff needed functions.

INTERPRETATION

Within both the public and private sectors, the percentage of students with College Work-Study (CWS) jobs tends to increase as tuition rises. Among private institutions, the percentage with CWS positions in the highest tuition category is nearly double that in the lowest tuition group. Within the public sector, twice the proportion of students in regional and research universities hold CWS jobs as students in two-year colleges. That CWS employment reflects student need relative to institutional charges is also evident in the fact that the overall percentages of CWS-employed students is significantly higher throughout the private sector than in any of the public sector groups.

PERCENT OF STUDENTS WITH COLLEGE WORK-STUDY JOBS

PUBLIC

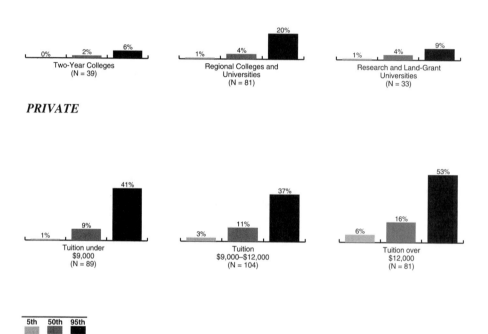

PRIVATE

QUESTIONS FOR POLICY MAKERS TO ASK

1. What have been the recent trends in College Work-Study employment at our institution?

2. Are we confident that we have done all we can to maximize the availability of CWS jobs for our students?

3. Have we been successful in parlaying the availability of CWS jobs at our institution into an advantage relative to the institutions with which we compete for students?

Tenure status of FTE faculty
Percent of FTE faculty who are non-tenured
Percent of FTE faculty who are tenured
Percent of FTE faculty who are non-tenure-line

SIGNIFICANCE

Many policy makers, including trustees and public officials, find the concept of tenure baffling and exasperating. How, they ask, can an institution ensure that it remains flexible, financially and programmatically, when a substantial portion of its most essential resource—the faculty—is virtually immovable? Proponents of tenure counter that the protections tenure affords are absolutely essential to the academic freedom that makes it possible to function as a faculty member.

Institutions have responded to the tenure question in a number of ways. While some have abandoned tenure altogether, most colleges and universities have maintained conventional tenure systems while at the same time devising variations and new practices aimed at providing more flexibility. For example, a growing number of institutions are establishing non-tenure-line (ineligible for tenure) positions, either temporary or on a longer-term contract basis. Some are establishing tenure quotas, raising standards for achieving tenure, or providing incentives to tenured faculty to retire.

Critics argue that such devices can be destructive. Tenure quotas can weaken faculty morale by foreclosing opportunities for permanent employment to even the most qualified individuals. Moreover, heavy reliance on temporary and contract faculty may compromise teaching quality and undermine faculty commitment to out-of-class activities such as student advising and faculty governance.

INTERPRETATION

Among private institutions the percentage of tenured faculty increases as tuition levels rise. Within the public sector, tenure levels are considerably higher in the regional and research university groups than among two-year colleges. The percentages of non-tenured (but tenure-eligible) faculty in private institutions decrease as tuition levels rise, suggesting that low-tuition institutions may be more likely to have younger faculty, tenure quotas, or more turnover among older, tenured faculty. A similar pattern holds among public institutions, with two-year colleges having the highest percentage of non-tenured (but tenure-eligible) faculty, and research universities the lowest.

Within the private sector, the low-tuition group is considerably more likely to have non-tenure-line faculty. Within the public sector, a similar pattern holds, with non-tenure-line faculty far more prevalent at two-year colleges than at regional and research universities.

TENURE STATUS OF FTE FACULTY

PUBLIC

PRIVATE

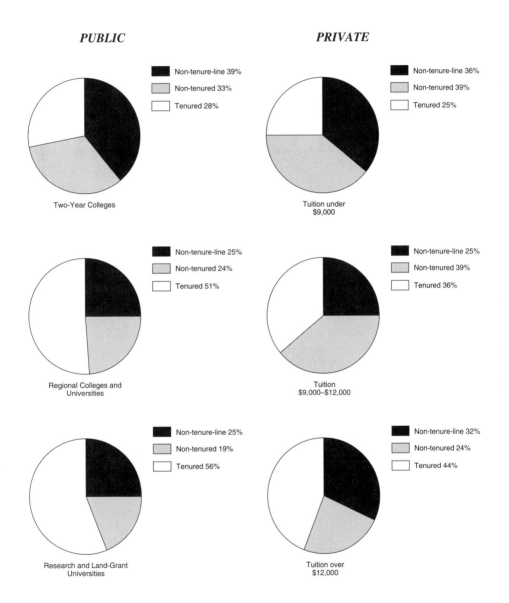

Non-tenure-line 39%
Non-tenured 33%
Tenured 28%

Two-Year Colleges

Non-tenure-line 36%
Non-tenured 39%
Tenured 25%

Tuition under
$9,000

Non-tenure-line 25%
Non-tenured 24%
Tenured 51%

Regional Colleges and
Universities

Non-tenure-line 25%
Non-tenured 39%
Tenured 36%

Tuition
$9,000–$12,000

Non-tenure-line 25%
Non-tenured 19%
Tenured 56%

Research and Land-Grant
Universities

Non-tenure-line 32%
Non-tenured 24%
Tenured 44%

Tuition over
$12,000

QUESTIONS FOR POLICY MAKERS TO ASK

1. What have been the recent trends in faculty tenure status at our institution?

2. Do we have any explicit or implicit policies or practices that limit the percentage of faculty eligible for tenure?

3. Is there any evidence that teaching quality or commitment to advising and other faculty responsibilities varies according to tenure status?

4. If recent tenure and faculty turnover trends were to continue over the next few years, what would be the implications for tenure levels within our faculty? What would be the implications for our budget?

5. What strategies can we adopt to ensure that we maintain necessary financial and programmatic flexibility while maintaining faculty morale and stability?

Percent of FTE faculty who are part-time

SIGNIFICANCE

The percentage of FTE faculty who are part-time often reflects an institutional policy to minimize costs or enhance staffing flexibility by avoiding long-term commitments to faculty. In some cases, an institution has little choice but to rely on part-time faculty, even if it might wish to do otherwise. For example, there are shortages of potential faculty in certain fields, often because there are more attractive employment opportunities available to them outside of higher education. Moreover, some institutional curricula are dominated by technical or professionally-oriented programs where professionals can make important contributions as teachers.

Generally, institutions with a higher percentage of part-time faculty have lower overall costs for faculty salaries and benefits. At the same time, over-reliance on part-time faculty may harm institutional morale, quality of teaching, and accessibility of faculty to students and the institution.

INTERPRETATION

In the public sector, dependence on part-time faculty decreases as institutional selectivity rises. That is, the percentage of part-time faculty at two-year colleges is more than six times that of research institutions. In part, this finding probably reflects the career orientation of most public two-year colleges, and hence the appropriateness of using working professionals as part-time instructors. Dependence on part-time faculty within the private sector is greater than at public regional and research institutions, though, within the private sector, it is lowest among the highest tuition institutions.

PERCENT OF FTE FACULTY WHO ARE PART-TIME

PUBLIC

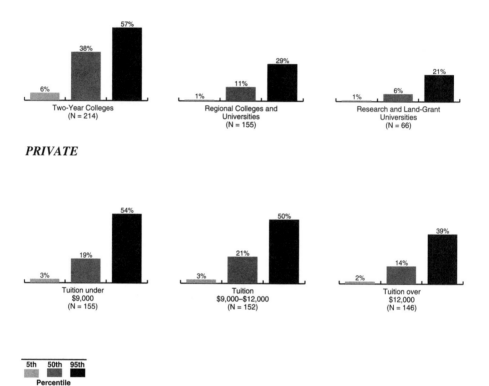

PRIVATE

QUESTIONS FOR POLICY MAKERS TO ASK

1. What have been the recent trends in employment of part-time faculty by our institution? Do these trends vary by program or department?

2. Why do we employ part-time rather than full-time faculty?

3. Is there any evidence that teaching quality or commitment to advising and other faculty responsibilities varies by full-time versus part-time status?

4. What strategies could we employ to enhance the commitment part-time faculty feel toward our institution and its students?

Women faculty
Percent of FTE faculty who are women
Percent of FTE female faculty by tenure status

SIGNIFICANCE

In recent years, many institutions have attempted to increase the number of women on their faculty. The percentage of FTE faculty at a college or university who are women may be a function of the program mix of the institution relative to the qualifications of potential women faculty, demand for faculty in fields that historically have attracted larger numbers of women, the success of affirmative action programs, the institution's geographic location, the historical and current mission of the institution, and the openness of the campus to diversity.

Once hired, the tenure status of women faculty is a function of the tenure policies and practices of the institution; the presence or absence of tenure quotas; faculty turnover prior to the tenure decision year; the percentage of faculty ineligible for tenure (temporary, part-time, contract faculty, and other non-tenure line faculty, for example); and the retirement and resignation rates of tenured faculty.

INTERPRETATION

The percentage of women faculty has increased substantially in recent years and now averages well over one-third across most institution types. The highest concentrations of women faculty are found in public two-year colleges and the lowest in public research universities. In both the public and private sectors, proportions of women faculty decline as institutional wealth, prestige, and selectivity increase.

Significantly higher proportions of women faculty in the public sector are tenured, compared with those in the private sector. Looking at the two sectors separately, percentages of women faculty who are tenured rise, in both public and private institutions, with institutional wealth, prestige, and selectivity. Percentages of non-tenure-eligible women faculty show the opposite pattern. That is, they decline in both sectors as institutional wealth, selectivity, and prestige rise. These findings may suggest greater confidence among wealthier institutions in their ability to sustain permanent faculty positions.

PERCENT OF FTE FACULTY WHO ARE WOMEN

PUBLIC

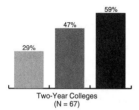

Two-Year Colleges
(N = 67)

29% 47% 59%

Regional Colleges and
Universities
(N = 87)

25% 37% 49%

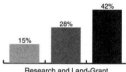

Research and Land-Grant
Universities
(N = 46)

15% 28% 42%

PRIVATE

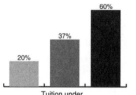

Tuition under
$9,000
(N = 46)

20% 37% 60%

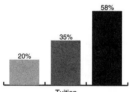

Tuition
$9,000–$12,000
(N = 74)

20% 35% 58%

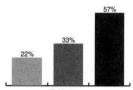

Tuition over
$12,000
(N = 72)

22% 33% 57%

5th   50th   95th
Percentile

PERCENT OF FTE FEMALE FACULTY BY TENURE STATUS

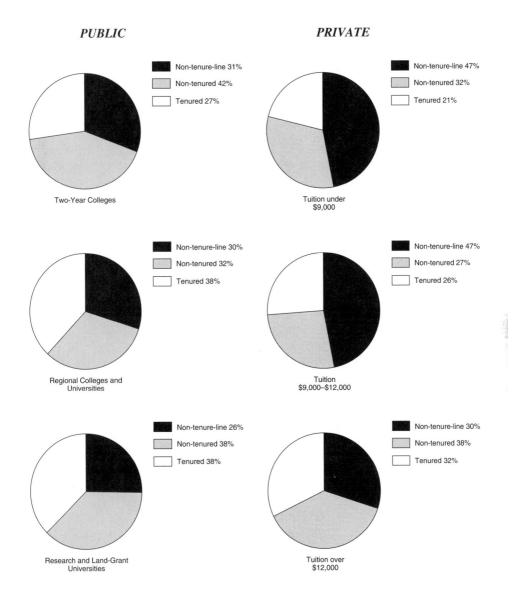

PUBLIC

PRIVATE

Non-tenure-line 31%
Non-tenured 42%
Tenured 27%

Two-Year Colleges

Non-tenure-line 47%
Non-tenured 32%
Tenured 21%

Tuition under
$9,000

Non-tenure-line 30%
Non-tenured 32%
Tenured 38%

Regional Colleges and
Universities

Non-tenure-line 47%
Non-tenured 27%
Tenured 26%

Tuition
$9,000–$12,000

Non-tenure-line 26%
Non-tenured 38%
Tenured 38%

Research and Land-Grant
Universities

Non-tenure-line 30%
Non-tenured 38%
Tenured 32%

Tuition over
$12,000

QUESTIONS FOR POLICY MAKERS TO ASK

1. What have been the recent trends in employment and tenure status of women faculty at our institution?

2. Do these trends reflect conscious institutional efforts, and are we satisfied with these efforts? If not, what corrective actions can we take?

3. Are the employment trends and the experiences of women faculty at our institution comparable to those of male faculty? If not, what accounts for these differences?

4. What efforts is the institution making to improve the campus climate for women faculty?

FTE faculty by racial/ethnic status

SIGNIFICANCE

The diversity of the American population has increased significantly in recent years, and many colleges and universities have been working harder to increase the diversity of their faculty, though numbers of minority faculty on most campuses are still very low.

The racial and ethnic makeup of the faculty is a function of the relationship of the institution's program mix to the supply of faculty, the success of affirmative action programs, institutional hiring practices and policies, the institution's geographical location, the historical and current mission of the institution, and the openness of the campus to diversity.

INTERPRETATION

The percentage of minority faculty within the public sector increases with institutional selectivity, wealth, and prestige, and, overall, percentages of minority faculty are higher in the public sector than among private institutions. Within the public sector, black faculty are slightly less likely to be found in research universities, which, on average, employ more Asian/Pacific Islander faculty than any other institutional group, public or private. Hispanic faculty are fewer in number than either black or Asian/Pacific Islander faculty.

Native Americans represent well under one percent of FTE faculty in all institutional categories and thus are not reported here.

FTE FACULTY BY RACIAL/ETHNIC STATUS

PUBLIC

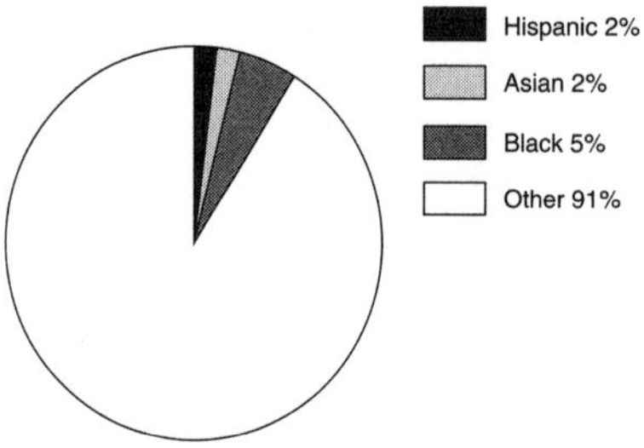

Hispanic 2%
Asian 2%
Black 5%
Other 91%

Two-Year Colleges

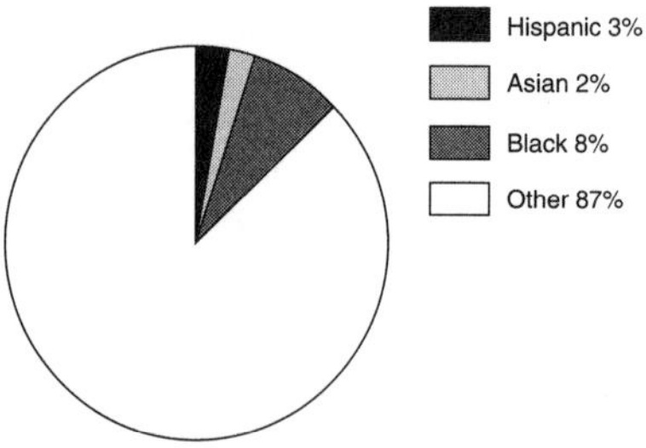

Hispanic 2%
Asian 4%
Black 6%
Other 88%

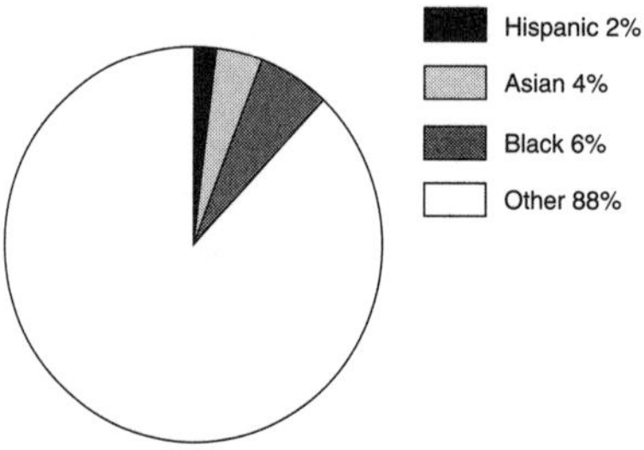

Regional Colleges and
Universities

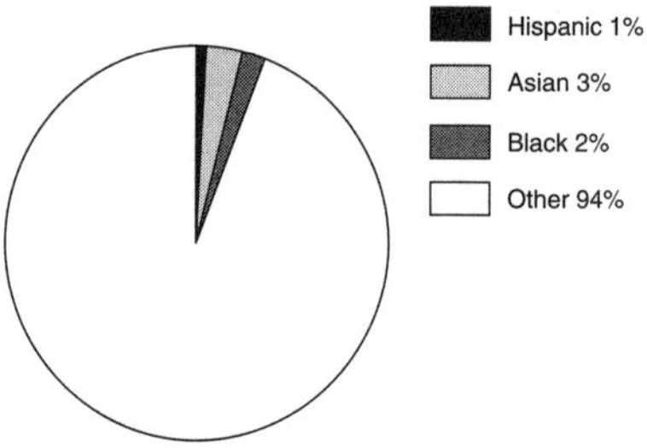

Hispanic 2%
Asian 7%
Black 5%
Other 86%

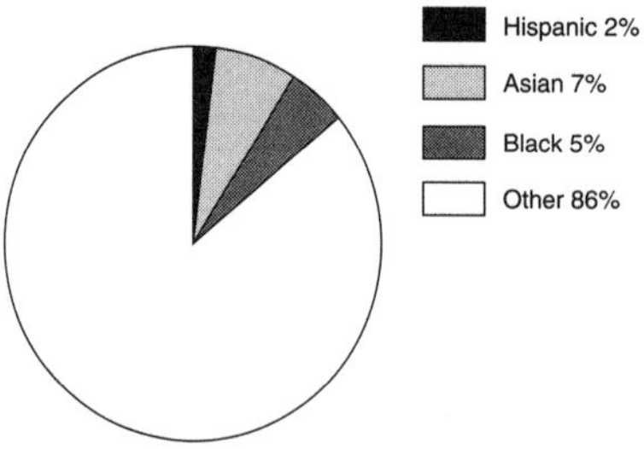

Research and Land-Grant
Universities

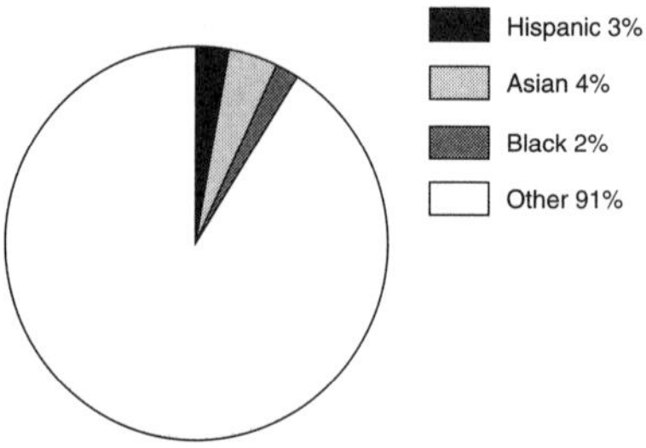

PRIVATE

Hispanic 3%
Asian 2%
Black 8%
Other 87%

Tuition under
$9,000

Hispanic 1%
Asian 3%
Black 2%
Other 94%

Tuition
$9,000–$12,000

Hispanic 3%
Asian 4%
Black 2%
Other 91%

Tuition over
$12,000

QUESTIONS FOR POLICY MAKERS TO ASK

1. What have been the recent trends in faculty employment by racial/ethnic status at our institution?

2. Do these trends reflect conscious institutional efforts, and are we satisfied with these efforts? If not, what corrective actions can we take?

3. Are the employment experiences of minority faculty at our institution comparable to those of non-minorities? If not, what accounts for these differences?

4. What efforts is the institution making to improve the campus climate for minority faculty?

Percent of full-time faculty who are over 60
Percent of part-time faculty who are over 60

SIGNIFICANCE

With the end of mandatory retirement, institutions should be monitoring the age distribution of their faculty. Because most older faculty have attained tenure, advanced rank, and greater seniority, they typically are paid more than younger faculty. To the extent that a college or university depends disproportionately on older faculty, it may have fewer resources to compensate younger faculty or hire new ones.

A rising percentage of full-time faculty who are older than 60 may suggest the need for incentives and other programs to encourage faculty to retire voluntarily. Some institutions are encouraging older faculty to retire by guaranteeing part-time employment for a period of time, by subsidizing the cost of medical and other benefits, by providing office or secretarial space, or by other means. In that regard, for some institutions, a declining percentage of older full-time faculty, accompanied by a rising percentage of older part-time faculty, may signal a positive trend. That is, the institution may be gaining needed flexibility while retaining the services and good will of experienced and committed older faculty.

INTERPRETATION

Roughly 9 to 11 percent of full-time faculty are older than 60 in all institution groups except two-year public colleges, where the figure is 6 percent. On average, full-time faculty in the private sector are older than public institution faculty. The opposite pattern is seen among part-time faculty over 60, who are more common in the public sector than in private institutions.

PERCENT OF FULL-TIME FACULTY OVER 60

PUBLIC

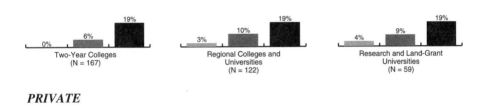

| Two-Year Colleges (N = 167) | Regional Colleges and Universities (N = 122) | Research and Land-Grant Universities (N = 59) |

0%   6%   19%   3%   10%   19%   4%   9%   19%

PRIVATE

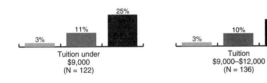
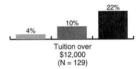

3%   11%   25%   3%   10%   21%   4%   10%   22%

| Tuition under $9,000 (N = 122) | Tuition $9,000–$12,000 (N = 136) | Tuition over $12,000 (N = 129) |

5th   50th   95th
Percentile

PERCENT OF PART-TIME FACULTY OVER 60

PUBLIC

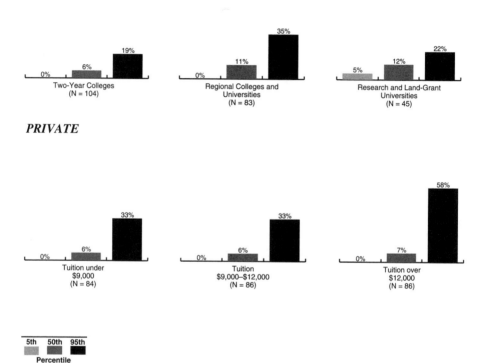

PRIVATE

5th 50th 95th
Percentile

QUESTIONS FOR POLICY MAKERS TO ASK

1. What have been the recent age distributions of faculty at our institution? Do we have more or fewer older faculty than in past years? Are older faculty broadly distributed or concentrated in a few departments?

2. Do we have any explicit or implicit policies or practices that encourage or discourage faculty retirement?

3. Is there any evidence that teaching quality or commitment to research or other faculty responsibilities changes as faculty grow older? If so, how should we respond?

4. If recent faculty age trends were to continue over the next few years, what would be the implications for salary and benefit costs and for employment opportunities for younger faculty?

5. What impact are we experiencing from changes in Federal law governing mandatory retirement?

Student-faculty ratios, overall and by academic major

Ratio of FTE students to FTE faculty
Ratio of FTE business administration majors to FTE business administration faculty
Ratio of FTE humanities majors to FTE humanities faculty
Ratio of FTE science/math FTE science/math faculty
Ratio of FTE social science majors to FTE social science faculty
Ratio of FTE health professions majors to FTE health professions faculty
Ratio of FTE engineering majors to FTE engineering faculty
Ratio of FTE education majors to FTE education faculty

SIGNIFICANCE

It is common to describe the productivity of an institution's faculty in terms of the overall ratio of students to faculty. In purely economic terms, a college with a 20:1 ratio is more productive than one whose ratio is 10:1, though it is often argued, accurately or not, that the institution with the lower ratio provides a better education.

Institution-wide student-faculty ratios may mask significant variations among programs, departments, or schools within an institution. For example, a university may have an overall ratio of 15:1 but schools within the university may vary between 5:1 and 40:1, depending on student demand for the schools' programs. Ratios can be calculated on the basis of numbers of student majors, as they are here, or according to production of student credit hours, as in the indicator described on page 166. The two measures differ to the extent that faculty in one field provide general education credits or other service to non-majors.

INTERPRETATION

Among both public and private institutions, as institutional selectivity and prestige increase, the overall student-faculty ratio declines. Overall, student-faculty ratios are higher in the public sector than in private institutions.

When analyzed by major field, large discrepancies in ratios become evident, though it is important to note that these data reflect only numbers of majors rather than credit hour production. In general, the highest average student-faculty ratios are seen in business administration and engineering programs. Health sciences and education majors also have relatively high student-faculty ratios. Ratios are lowest in the humanities and in science and mathematics.

RATIOS OF FTE STUDENTS TO FTE FACULTY

	Public Two-year	*Public Regional Colleges and Universities*	*Public Research and Land-Grant Universities*	*Private tuition under $9,000*	*Private tuition $9,000– $12,000*	*Private tuition over $12,000*
Business	19:1	23:1	23:1	20:1	16:1	15:1
Education	29:1	18:1	12:1	12:1	12:1	7:1
Engineering	25:1	17:1	17:1	15:1	12:1	12:1
Health professions	15:1	19:1	4:1	16:1	9:1	4:1
Humanities	10:1	7:1	7:1	5:1	5:1	6:1
Science/Math	18:1	10:1	9:1	8:1	7:1	7:1
Social Science	10:1	14:1	14:1	12:1	9:1	9:1

QUESTIONS FOR POLICY MAKERS TO ASK

1. What have been the recent trends in student-faculty ratios at our institution, overall and by major program?

2. Do these trends suggest that we have too many or too few faculty or students in some of our programs? If so, how should we respond?

3. Is there any evidence that particularly high or low student-faculty ratios are having a negative effect on teaching quality, student satisfaction, or faculty morale?

Faculty credit hour production

Credit hour production per FTE faculty member, by
department/division:
Business administration
Humanities
Science/math
Social science
Health professions
Engineering
Education

SIGNIFICANCE

Along with departmental student-faculty ratios, credit hour production by department is a measure of faculty productivity. The latter measure provides a more complete picture than the former because it reflects the extent to which faculty in one field provide general education credits or other service to non-majors. This is particularly important in fields such as the humanities, sciences, and social sciences, since most departments in these areas provide a substantial number of "service courses" to students majoring in other fields.

Credit hour production rises or falls with changes in class size and in numbers of courses taught. That is, an individual faculty member may teach a total of 150 students in a single lecture course, in three separate courses, or in three sections of the same course. While credit hour production would be identical in all three cases, teaching three separate courses arguably involves the greatest actual workload.

As with student-faculty ratios, institution-wide measures of credit hour production may mask significant variations among programs, departments, or schools within an institution. So too is there controversy about the tradeoff between high credit hour production and academic quality.

INTERPRETATION

Viewed in conjunction with ratios of student academic majors to FTE faculty, the effects of service courses and general education requirements are obvious. While ratios of majors in the humanities and in science and math are relatively low, credit hour production in these two areas is higher than in, for example, the health professions, engineering, and education, which have more majors but provide fewer service courses.

Very low numbers of credit hours produced in some fields, such as health professions in private sector institutions, suggest that faculty in those programs may teach only some of their courses in that major and others in allied disciplines such as science.

Credit hour production is significantly higher in public institutions than private colleges and universities. Overall, private institutions are much smaller than publics, many of them view small classes as a virtue, and others are experiencing declining enrollments. Therefore, private institutions may believe they must employ relatively more faculty to provide comprehensive academic offerings, and perhaps even retain more faculty—many of them tenured—than a declining student body would justify.

FACULTY CREDIT HOUR PRODUCTION PER FTE FACULTY BY DEPARTMENT/DIVISION

	Public Two-year	*Public Regional Colleges and Universities*	*Public Research and Land-Grant Universities*	*Private tuition under $9,000*	*Private tuition $9,000–$12,000*	*Private tuition over $12,000*
Business	691	581	651	343	348	291
Education	733	549	433	254	322	206
Engineering	463	456	340	89	199	204
Health professions	507	405	151	184	188	43
Humanities	562	518	506	257	277	215
Science/Math	1,105	650	584	287	300	224
Social Science	820	731	704	326	352	247

QUESTIONS FOR POLICY MAKERS TO ASK

1. What have been the recent trends in credit-hour production at our institution?

2. Do these trends suggest that we have too many or too few faculty or students in some of our programs? If so, how should we respond?

3. Is there any evidence of erosion in teaching quality, student satisfaction, or faculty morale within departments/divisions that produce a particularly high or low number of credit hours?

Faculty headcount in Fall, 1994 as a percent of faculty headcount in Fall, 1993
FTE faculty in Fall, 1994 as a percent of FTE faculty in Fall, 1993

SIGNIFICANCE

Because faculty provide an institution's core services, and because compensation absorbs such a large percentage of operating revenues, institutions should monitor changes in faculty headcounts and FTEs. Changes may result from a variety of factors, including resource availability, the availability of prospective faculty, rates of retirement, decisions to grant or deny tenure or reappointment, and voluntary departures by faculty.

Changes in faculty size should be evaluated in the context of changes in student enrollment and availability of resources. A faculty that grows in proportion to student enrollment and revenue increases may suggest good institutional condition, while a steady faculty in an institution experiencing either losses or gains in enrollment and revenues may be cause for concern. For example, among public institutions experiencing declining appropriations, it is common to see a constant faculty with a rising student body. Among some other institutions, both public and private, tenure commitments may result in a fixed faculty as enrollments decline.

Typically, changes in faculty size vary among departments and programs. That is, a faculty that is unchanged overall may be experiencing significant increases and decreases within individual units of the institution.

It is wise to review changes in both FTE and headcount faculty. For example, a steady-state headcount may mask large increases in dependence on part-time faculty. If so, that change will be revealed by the FTE figure.

INTERPRETATION

On average, both faculty headcount and FTE faculty grew very slightly during the period studied, more so among private institutions than public colleges and universities. Headcounts grew slightly more than FTEs, indicating that at least some of this modest growth was due to the addition of part-time faculty.

FACULTY HEADCOUNT IN FALL, 1994 AS A PERCENT OF FACULTY HEADCOUNT IN FALL, 1993

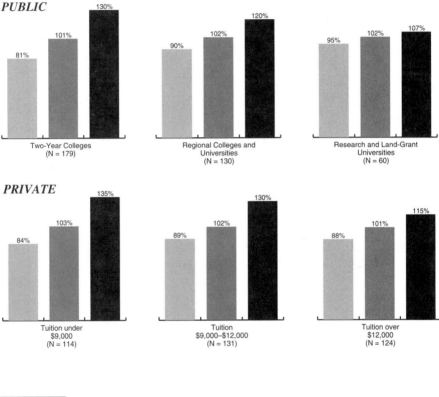

PUBLIC

Two-Year Colleges
(N = 179)
81% 101% 130%

Regional Colleges and
Universities
(N = 130)
90% 102% 120%

Research and Land-Grant
Universities
(N = 60)
95% 102% 107%

PRIVATE

Tuition under
$9,000
(N = 114)
84% 103% 135%

Tuition
$9,000–$12,000
(N = 131)
89% 102% 130%

Tuition over
$12,000
(N = 124)
88% 101% 115%

5th   50th   95th
Percentile

FTE FACULTY IN FALL, 1994 AS A PERCENT OF FTE FACULTY IN FALL, 1993

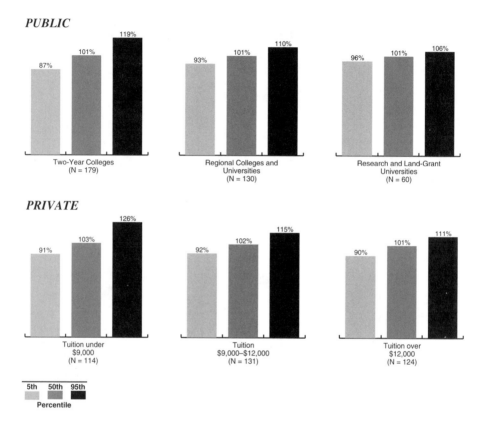

PUBLIC

Two-Year Colleges (N = 179): 87%, 101%, 119%

Regional Colleges and Universities (N = 130): 93%, 101%, 110%

Research and Land-Grant Universities (N = 60): 96%, 101%, 106%

PRIVATE

Tuition under $9,000 (N = 114): 91%, 103%, 126%

Tuition $9,000–$12,000 (N = 131): 92%, 102%, 115%

Tuition over $12,000 (N = 124): 90%, 101%, 111%

5th 50th 95th
Percentile

QUESTIONS FOR POLICY MAKERS TO ASK

1. What have been the recent trends in faculty employment at our institution, both in terms of headcounts and FTEs?

2. Do these trends reflect conscious institutional policy and practice, or have they occurred more or less by accident?

3. Have changes in faculty employment related in any way to changes in student enrollments? Are there areas where enrollments or other institutional needs suggest we need more or fewer faculty?

4. Have faculty employment trends varied by department, program, or school?

Percentage of total FTE employees who are faculty

SIGNIFICANCE

The proportion of employees who are faculty reflects an institution's academic focus, as well as its choices about the division of labor between faculty and staff. Over the past few decades, institutions have added professional staff in areas such as admissions and advising, where previously faculty performed these duties. Other technical and administrative positions have been added to support faculty work in research-intensive institutions. Institutions also may choose to leverage faculty time by adding support staff in areas such as student services, admissions, and information technology. Whether such leverage boosts or depresses overall institutional productivity depends on what faculty do with their excess time, relative to the institution's mission and goals. For example, if the extra time is used to teach or advise more students, do research, or develop new courses, overall institutional productivity will rise, even if such productivity gains are difficult to measure and quantify.

INTERPRETATION

As institutional wealth and selectivity increase, the proportion of FTE employees who are faculty declines. In the private sector, faculty employment declines as tuition rises. Among public institutions, the percentage of community college employees who are faculty is more than 50 percent and declines to 30 percent in research universities, possibly because of their public service and research commitments.

PERCENTAGE OF TOTAL FTE EMPLOYEES WHO ARE FACULTY

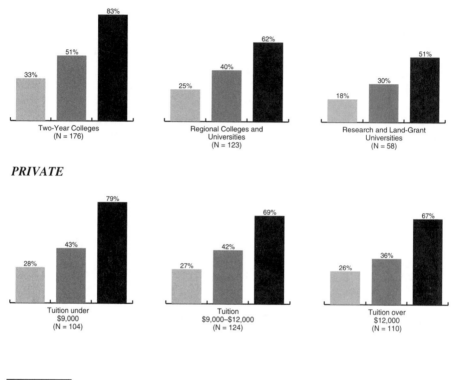

PUBLIC

Two-Year Colleges
(N = 176)

33% 51% 83%

Regional Colleges and Universities
(N = 123)

25% 40% 62%

Research and Land-Grant Universities
(N = 58)

18% 30% 51%

PRIVATE

Tuition under $9,000
(N = 104)

28% 43% 79%

Tuition $9,000–$12,000
(N = 124)

27% 42% 69%

Tuition over $12,000
(N = 110)

26% 36% 67%

5th 50th 95th
Percentile

QUESTIONS FOR POLICY MAKERS TO ASK

1. What have been the recent trends in faculty and non-faculty employment at our institution?

2. In what areas has non-faculty employment increased or decreased? what explains these changes?

3. If recent employment trends were to continue over the next few years, what would be the implications for our ability to provide instruction, research, and administrative support?

4. Are we satisfied with our faculty-to-staff ratio? How can we begin to make any adjustments that appear to be required?

Percent of total FTE employees who are executive, administrative, and managerial staff

SIGNIFICANCE

The proportion of employees who are classified as executive, administrative, or managerial can be a function of the institution's emphasis on administration, oversight, and other professional activities versus functions typically performed by faculty or by clerical and other non-exempt staff. A high proportion of professional and managerial staff can also indicate that the institution has the relatively greater financial ability required to pay the higher salaries associated with professional and managerial positions or that the complexities of certain institutions require a greater proportion of relatively higher level staff.

INTERPRETATION

Overall, the percentage of total employees who are classified as executive, administrative, and managerial is significantly higher in the private sector. This may be due to the smaller average size of private institutions, which deny them the economies of scale in administrative staffing that are available to the much larger public institutions. Within the private sector, this indicator does not vary by tuition level, suggesting that the availability of more resources does not cause an institution to hire relatively more managerial employees. Within the public sector, the percentage of executive, administrative, and managerial staff is smallest in research universities, which are larger than either two-year colleges or regional institutions, again reinforcing the notion that economies of scale may enable an institution to employ relatively fewer managers.

PERCENT OF TOTAL FTE EMPLOYEES WHO ARE EXECUTIVE, ADMINISTRATIVE, AND MANAGERIAL STAFF

PUBLIC

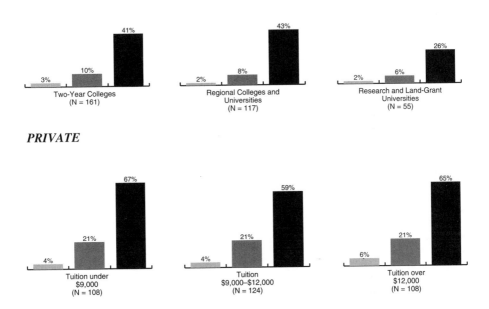

PRIVATE

QUESTIONS FOR POLICY MAKERS TO ASK

1. What have been the recent trends in professional and managerial employment at our institution?

2. In what areas has professional and managerial employment increased or decreased? what explains these changes?

3. If recent employment trends were to continue over the next few years, what would be the implications for our ability to provide appropriate administrative oversight and services? How can we begin to make any adjustments that appear to be required?

Notes on the Survey

The indicator values reported in this book are based on the results of a national survey of 992 colleges and universities. The survey was mailed in November 1995, and a follow-up letter was mailed to nonrespondents in January 1996. The survey was directed to the president's office, with the suggestion that it be completed by the institutional research office or by others with access to the required data.

To enhance the accuracy of data reported in the book, we requested raw numbers rather than percentages, and we calculated the indicators from those data. The questions from the survey instrument and a glossary of terms are included on pages 178–192. The data items included in each indicator and the formulas used to calculate the indicators are described beginning on page 193.

SURVEY RESPONSE RATES, BY INSTITUTION TYPE

Institution Type	Surveys Mailed	Responses Received	Percent Response
Public			
Two-year Colleges	914	251	27%
Regional Colleges and Universities[1]	321	181	56%
Research and Land-Grant Universities[2]	152	76	50%
Private			
Tuition under $9,000	389	155	40%
Tuition $9,000–$12,000	293	169	58%
Tuition over $12,000	303	160	53%

[1]This category includes colleges and universities eligible for membership in the American Association of State Colleges and Universities.

[2]This category includes universities eligible for membership in the National Association of State Universities and Land-Grant Colleges or the Association of American Universities.

SURVEY OF STRATEGIC INDICATORS

FOR HIGHER EDUCATION-1995

Peterson's Guides and AGB Research Survey

I.   FINANCIAL PROFILE

A. Revenues

**1994/1995 Fiscal Year
Total Dollars**

1. Tuition and fees	1
2. Sales and services of educational activities	2
3. Auxiliary enterprises	3
4. Hospitals	4
5. Other sources	5
6. Independent operations	6
7. Government appropriations	
a. Federal	7a
b. State	7b
c. Local	7c
8. Government grants and contracts	
a. Federal	8a
b. State	8b
c. Local	8c
9. Private gifts, grants, and contracts	9
10. Endowment support for operations	10

B. Expenditures

**1994/1995 Fiscal Year
Total Dollars**

1. Instruction	1
2. Sponsored research	2
3. Public service	3
4. Academic support (total)	4
a. Libraries (included in 4, Academic support)	4a
b. Academic computing (included in 4, Academic support)	4b
5. Student services (excluding student financial aid awards)	5
6. Institutional support	6
7. Plant operations and maintenance	7
8. Mandatory transfers	8

	1994/1995 Fiscal Year Total Dollars

9. Auxiliary enterprises	9
10. Hospitals	10
11. Independent operations	11
12. Scholarships and fellowships	12
a. Institutional scholarships and fellowships (included in 12, Scholarships & fellowships)	12 a

	1994/1995 Fiscal Year Total Dollars

C. Assets, Liabilities, Fund Balances

1. Current fund balance 1994–95	1
2. Current fund balance 1993–94	2
3. Unexpended plant funds balance	3
4. Beginning-of-year market value of endowment	
a. *Pure + term*	4a
b. *Quasi*	4b
5. End-of-year market value of endowment	
a. *Pure + term*	5a
b. *Quasi*	5b
6. Endowment yield	6
7. *Total return on endowment*	7
8. *Total liabilities*	8
9. *Short-term debt*	9
10. *Long-term debt*	10
11. *Total assets*	11

D. Fund-Raising   **A note to public institutions: Please report all fund-raising results, whether they were undertaken directly by the institution or by separately incorporated foundations. Most data categories are consistent with those used by the Council for Aid to Education (CFAE).**

	1994/1995 Fiscal Year Total Dollars

1. *Gift income from alumni*	1
2. *Gift income from parents*	2
3. *Gift income from other individuals*	3
4. That portion of gift income reported in 1, 2, & 3 above that comes from *trustees* (including foundation trustees)	4
5. *Gift income from private foundations*	5
6. *Gift income from corporations*	6

	1994/1995 Fiscal Year **Total Dollars**
7. *Gift income from religious organizations*	7
8. *Gift income from fund-raising consortia*	8
9. *Gift income from other organizations*	9
10. *Bequests received*	10
11. Planned gifts	
a. *Market value of new gifts*	11a
b. *Net realizable value of new gifts*	11b
12. Percent of living alumni who have given at any time in the past five years.	12 _____ %

II. PHYSICAL PLANT DETAIL

1994/1995 Fiscal Year
Total Dollars

1. *Beginning of year replacement value of plant*
2. End-of-year replacement value of plant
3. *Estimated maintenance backlog of plant*
4. Replacement value of new investment in plant

Replacement Value	**Book Value**

5. *Plant depreciation identified during the year*

III. LIBRARY AND INFORMATION RESOURCES

1994/1995 Fiscal Year
Total Dollars

A. Library Resources

1. Total number of book and monograph volumes (all libraries)   A1

B. Organization and Financing

1. Does the institution have a "Chief Information Officer" who is responsible for both institution strategic data and academic information resources (including libraries)? ☐Yes   ☐No

   a. If yes, to whom does this person report? (title only)_____

2. Does the institution have a formal policy, in place now, for funding the *depreciation of computer equipment*? ☐Yes   ☐No

   a. If yes, what is the *depreciation period* (in years)? _____

C. Computer network information

1. Does the institution have a *campus-wide network* installed and operational?   ☐ Yes   ☐No

   a. If yes, is the *central spine of the campus-wide network*: ☐*Fiber optic*   ☐*Coaxial cable*   ☐*Other*

   b. Is the library catalog on the campus-wide network? ☐Yes   ☐No

   c. Approximately what percentage of the following facilities have connections to this network?

Administrative offices	_____ %	Classrooms/labs	_____ %
Faculty/staff offices	_____ %	Student rooms	_____ %
Libraries	_____ %	Student dormitories	_____ %

2. If the institution has a campus-wide network installed and operational, does it provide: (check one)

☐ Full access to the Internet (e.g., wide-band access capable of using the graphical capabilities of World Wide Web).

☐ Partial access to the Internet (e.g., for electronic mail only)

☐ No access to the Internet (other than, for example, dial-up from individual workstations)

3. If the institution has a connection to the Internet,

a. What is the *bandwidth of the Internet connection*:   _____

b. Which of the following Internet services are available? (check all that apply)

☐ E-mail   ☐ FTP   ☐ News Lists

☐ Gopher   ☐ Telnet   ☐ List Serves

D. Student computers

1. Total number of personal computers and/or terminals supplied for student use: D1 [   ]

2. Does the institution require entering **full-time** undergraduates to have computers? ☐Yes   ☐No

a. If yes, are the costs for computers included in tuition and fees, or paid by a separate but required charge?

☐Included   ☐Separate

3. Does the institution require entering **part-time** undergraduates to have computers?   ☐Yes   ☐No

a. If yes, are the costs for computers included in tuition and fees, or paid by a separate but required charge?

☐Included   ☐Separate

IV. STUDENT PROFILE

A. Enrollment

1. Full-time undergraduate freshman admission for Fall 1994

a. Number of **completed** undergraduate *freshman applicants* 1a

b. Undergraduate *freshman applicants accepted* 1b

c. Accepted undergraduate *freshman applicants who matriculated* 1c

FALL 1994 HEADCOUNT

2. Full-time transfer undergraduate admission for Fall 1994

a. Number of **completed** *transfer undergraduate applicants* 2a

b. *Transfer undergraduate applicants accepted* 2b

c. *Transfer undergraduate applicants who matriculated* 2c

FALL 1994 HEADCOUNT

3. Total full-time undergraduate students

4. Total full-time post-baccalaureate students

5. Total part-time undergraduate students

6. Total part-time post-baccalaureate students

7. Enrollment by student *degree level*

  a. *Associate*

  b. *Baccalaureate*

  c. *Master's*

  d. *Doctoral*

  e. *First-professional*

8. Enrollment by race/ethnicity of <u>undergraduates</u>
   (U.S. citizens and resident aliens only)

  a. Black, non-Hispanic

  b. Native American

  c. Asian or Pacific Islander

  d. Hispanic

  e. White, non-Hispanic

  f. Race/ethnicity unknown

9. Enrollment by race/ethnicity of <u>post-baccalaureate</u> students
   (U.S. citizens and resident aliens only)

  a. Black, non-Hispanic

  b. Native American

  c. Asian or Pacific Islander

  d. Hispanic

  e. White, non-Hispanic

  f. Race/ethnicity unknown

10. Female undergraduate students

11. Male undergraduate students

12. Female post-baccalaureate students

13. Male post-baccalaureate students

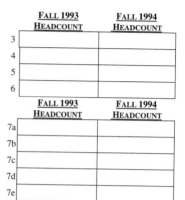

	FALL 1993 HEADCOUNT	FALL 1994 HEADCOUNT
3		
4		
5		
6		

	FALL 1993 HEADCOUNT	FALL 1994 HEADCOUNT
7a		
7b		
7c		
7d		
7e		

	FALL 1994 Full-time Headcount	Part-time Headcount
8a		
8b		
8c		
8d		
8e		
8f		

	FALL 1994 Full-time Headcount	Part-time Headcount
9a		
9b		
9c		
9d		
9e		
9f		
10		
11		
12		
13		

Survey of Strategic Indicators

14.   Enrollment by selected <u>undergraduate</u> majors

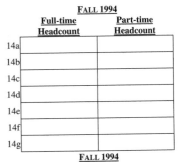

	FALL 1994	
	Full-time Headcount	**Part-time Headcount**
a. Business administration	14a	
b. Humanities	14b	
c. Science/mathematics	14c	
d. Social science	14d	
e. Health professions	14e	
f. Engineering	14f	
g. Education	14g	

15. Enrollment by selected <u>post-baccalaureate</u> majors

	FALL 1994	
	Full-time Headcount	**Part-time Headcount**
a. Business administration	15a	
b. Humanities	15b	
c. Science/mathematics	15c	
d. Social science	15d	
e. Health professions	15e	
f. Engineering	15f	
g. Education	15g	
16. *In-state undergraduate students enrolled*	16	
17. Undergraduate *students from outside the U.S. and Canada enrolled*	17	
18. *In-state post-baccalaureate students enrolled*	18	
19. Post-baccalaureate *students from outside the U.S. and Canada enrolled*	19	

20. Financial aid headcounts   (all students)

	FALL 1994	
	Full-time Headcount	**Part-time Headcount**
a. Students with *institutional scholarships and grants*	20a	
b. Students with *institutional loans*	20b	
c. Students with Federal Work-Study jobs	20c	

6

B. Degrees

1. Number of degrees awarded during the 1994–95 fiscal year

   a. *Associate*

   b. *Baccalaureate*

   c. *Master's*

   d. *Doctorate*

   e. *First-professional*

	1994/1995 FISCAL YEAR
1a	
1b	
1c	
1d	
1e	

V. FACULTY AND STAFF

A. Faculty Counts—Fall 1994

		FALL 1994	
		Full-time Headcount	Part-time Headcount
1. *Faculty* headcount (unduplicated, not FTE)	1		
a. *Tenured faculty*	1a		
b. *Non-tenured faculty*	1b		
c. *Non-tenure line faculty*	1c		
2. Female faculty by tenure status			
a. Tenured female faculty	2a		
b. Non-tenured female faculty	2b		
c. Non-tenure line female faculty	2c		
3. Faculty by race/ethnicity (U.S. citizens and resident aliens only)			
a. Black, non-Hispanic	3a		
b. Native American	3b		
c. Asian or Pacific Islander	3c		
d. Hispanic	3d		
e. White, non-Hispanic	3e		
f. Race/ethnicity unknown	3f		
4. Faculty who are over 60 years of age	4		
5. *Executive, administrative, and managerial staff*	5		
6. *Total employees*	6		

7. *Faculty by selected department/divisions.* Use "unduplicated" headcounts according to faculty member's primary area of teaching and/or research.

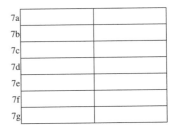

	FALL 1994	
	Full-time Headcount	**Part-time Headcount**
7a. Business administration		
7b. Humanities		
7c. Science/mathematics		
7d. Social science		
7e. Health professions		
7f. Engineering		
7g. Education		

B. Faculty Counts—Fall 1993

1. *Faculty* headcount **Fall 1993** (unduplicated, not FTE)

	FALL 1993	
	Full-time Headcount	**Part-time Headcount**
1		
1a. *Tenured faculty*		
1b. *Non-tenured faculty*		
1c. *Non-tenure line faculty*		

C. Credit hour Production

1. *Total credit hours produced by selected departments/divisions* in fiscal year 1994–95

	1994/1995 FISCAL YEAR
1a. Business administration	
1b. Humanities	
1c. Science/mathematics	
1d. Social science	
1e. Health professions	
1f. Engineering	
1g. Education	

VI. SPONSORED RESEARCH

A. *Sources of Funds Expended for Sponsored Research*

	1994/1995 FISCAL YEAR	
	Unrestricted	**Restricted**
1. U.S. Government	1	
2. State and local government	2	
3. U.S. corporations	3	
4. Private U.S. foundations	4	
5. Bequests and gifts from living individuals	5	
6. Foreign governments, private foundations, and corporations	6	
7. Other outside sponsors	7	
8. Institutional funds	8	

GLOSSARY

1. **Academic computing (expenditures):** That portion of academic support expenditures used to support computing in the academic area (instruction, research, and public service).

2. **Academic support (expenditures):** Expenditures for the support services that are an integral part of the institution's primary mission of instruction, research and public service. Includes expenditures for libraries, museums, galleries, audiovisual services, academic computing support, ancillary support, academic administration, personnel development, and course and curriculum development. Also includes expenditures for veterinary and dental clinics if their primary purpose is to support the institutional program.

3. **Auxiliary enterprises (expenditures):** Expenditures for essentially self-supporting operations of the institution that exist to furnish a service to students, faculty or staff, and that charge a fee that is directly related to, although not necessarily equal to, the cost of the service. Examples are residence halls, food services, student health services, college stores, and barber shops.

4. **Bandwidth of the Internet connection:** The number of bits of data that can move across the connection in a given second (expressed as bits per second, bps, or baud).

5. **Beginning-of-year market value of endowment:** If the market value of some investments is not available, use whatever value was assigned by the institution in reporting market values in the annual financial report.

6. **Beginning-of-year** *or* **end-of-year replacement value of plant:** The cost at the beginning or end of the fiscal year to replace all buildings owned, rented, or used by the institution. Includes recent appraisal value or what is currently carried as insurance replacement value. Excludes the replacement values of those buildings which are a part of endowment or other capital fund investments in real estate. This figure is not a book value figure.

7. **Book and monograph volumes:** Non-periodical printed publications bound in hard or soft covers, or in loose-leaf format, of at least 49 pages, exclusive of the cover pages, or a juvenile non-periodical publication of any length bound in hard or soft covers.

8. **Campus-wide network:** The linkage of personal and other computers and peripherals (e.g., printers) across all or most of the campus for users to share peripherals, to draw on the resources of a file server to share programs and data, and to communicate with each other via electronic mail.

9. **Central spine of the campus-wide network:** The type of wiring linking the personal and other computers in the network.

10. **Coaxial cable:** A cable of an insulated wire surrounded by a solid or mesh metal wire for the high-capacity transmission of electrical impulses.

11. **Current fund balance:** Assets minus liabilities in the current fund. Current funds are those available for current operations, whether unrestricted or restricted.

12. **Degrees awarded:** Numbers of degrees awarded at each of the following levels:

    a. **Associate:** An award that normally requires at least 2 but less than 4 years of full-time equivalent college work.

    b. **Baccalaureate:** An award that normally requires at least 4 but not more than 5 years of full-time equivalent college-level work. Includes all bachelor's degrees conferred in a 5-year cooperative (work-study) program.

    c. **Master's:** An award that requires completion of a program of study of at least the full-time equivalent of 1 but not more than 2 academic years of work beyond the baccalaureate degree.

    d. **First Professional:** An award that requires completion of a program that meets all of the following criteria: 1) completion of the academic requirements to begin practice in the profession; 2) at least 2 years of college work prior to entering the program; 3) a total of at least 6 academic years of college work to complete the degree program, including prior required college work plus the length of the professional program itself. Includes degrees in areas such as chiropractic, dentistry, medicine, optometry, pharmacy, veterinary medicine, law, theology.

    e. **Doctorate:** The highest award a student can earn for graduate study. Includes such degrees as Doctor of Education,
        Doctor of Juridical Science, Doctor of Public Health, and Doctor of Philosophy.

13. **Degree level:** See definitions under "degrees awarded."

14. **Depreciation of computer equipment:** Apportionment of the cost of computer equipment as an annual expense arising out of the continuous lessening in the value of the equipment caused by wear and tear, the effects of the elements, and gradual obsolescence.

15. **Depreciation period of computer equipment:** The estimated useful life of computer equipment, over which time annual expenses are charged, up to the full cost of the equipment.

16. **End of year replacement value of plant:** See "beginning-of-year replacement value of plant."

17. **Endowment support for operations (revenues):** Income and appreciation of endowment (pure, quasi, and term) used to fund current operations.

18. **Endowment yield:** Earnings (not realized gains) on investments of endowments regardless of distribution made of the earnings to various institutional funds. Includes interest, dividends, rents, royalties, and amortization of purchased discounts and premiums.

19. **Estimated maintenance backlog of plant:** The institution's best estimate of the dollar value of deferred maintenance on existing physical plant. Includes all buildings owned by the institution. Excludes buildings that are part of endowment or other capital fund investments in real estate.

20. **Executive, administrative, and managerial staff:** Persons whose assignments require primary (and major) responsibility for management of the institution, or a customarily recognized department or subdivision thereof. Assignments require the performance of work directly related to management policies or general business operations of the institution, department, or subdivision. It is assumed that assignments in this category customarily and regularly require the incumbent to exercise discretion and independent judgment, and to direct the work of others. Included in this category are all officers holding titles such as president, vice president, dean, director, or the equivalent, as well as officers subordinate to any of these administrators with such titles as associate dean, assistant dean, executive officer of academic departments (department heads, or the equivalent) if their principal activity is administrative. (Note: Includes supervisors of professional employees, while supervisors of nonprofessional employees (technical, clerical, craft, and service/maintenance force) are to be reported within the specific categories of the personnel they supervise.)

21. **Expendable plant funds:** Unexpended plant funds, funds for renewal and replacement, and funds for retirement of indebtedness.

22. **Faculty:** Persons whose specific assignments customarily are made for the purpose of conducting instruction, research, or public service as a principal activity (or activities), and who hold academic-rank titles of professor, associate professor, assistant professor, instructor, lecturer, or the equivalent of any of these academic ranks. If their principal activity is instruction, this category includes deans, directors, or the equivalent, as well as associate deans, assistant deans, and executive officers of academic departments (chairpersons, heads, or the equivalent). Student teachers or research assistants are not included in this category.

23. **Faculty by selected departments/divisions:** Full-time and part-time headcounts of faculty according to their primary area of teaching and/or research.

24. **Faculty by race/ethnicity:** See "students by race/ethnicity" for definitions of racial/ethnic categories.

25. **Fiber optic:** A cable of very thin glass wire designed for the transmission of light impulses and, as a result, large amounts of data.

26. **Freshman applicants:** Students applying for full-time admission to an institution for the first time at the undergraduate level. Includes students applying for the fall term who attend college for the first time in the prior summer term. Also includes students who apply for advanced standing (college credits earned before graduation from high school.)

27. **Freshman applicants accepted:** Students accepted for full-time admission for the first at the undergraduate level; includes students applying for the fall term who attend college for the first time in the prior summer term; also includes students admitted for advanced standing (college credits earned before graduation from high school.)

28. **Freshman applicants who matriculated:** Entering freshmen who have never attended any college and who are enrolled for 12 or more semester credits; or 12 or more quarter credits; or 24 contact hours a week each term. Includes students enrolled full-time in the fall term who attended college for the first time in the prior summer term, and full-time students who entered with advanced standing (college credits earned before graduation from high school).

29. **Full-time equivalent:** the sum of all full-time headcount students or faculty members, plus one-third of all part-time headcount students or faculty members.

30. **Full-time students:**
    a. **Undergraduate:** a student enrolled for 12 or more semester credits, or 12 or more quarter credits, or 24 contact hours a week each term; a student enrolled in a 4-year or 5-year bachelor's degree program, in an associate's degree program, or in a vocational or technical program below the baccalaureate;
    b. **Graduate:** A student enrolled for 9 or more semester credits, or 9 or more quarter credits or students involved in thesis or dissertation preparation that are considered full time by the institution.

31. **Gift income:** The market or fair dollar value of all gifts actually received by the institution during the year. Includes cash, securities, property, and products. Sources include:
    a. **Alumni:** Former students—full- or part-time, undergraduate or graduate—who have earned some credit toward one of the degrees offered by the reporting institution. Examples: for the purpose of this survey, an individual who completed only one semester or, indeed, only one degree-credit course with passing grades may be included in the alumni category. An individual who matriculated but did not complete the semester or who enrolled in a special course that did not carry degree credit, offered, for example, through the institution's extension division, should not be included in the alumni category.
    b. **Parents:** Persons other than those defined as alumni who are the parents, grandparents, or guardians of either currently enrolled or former students of the reporting institution. An affiliation as an alumnus should take precedence over that of a parent for the purpose of this survey.
    c. **Other individuals:** All persons who are not classifiable as alumni or parents.
    d. **Trustees:** Individuals who are current or past members of the institution's governing board.
    e. **Private foundations:** Private tax-exempt entities, whether corporate or trust in legal form, that have been established and are operated exclusively for charitable purposes. (Note: Not all grant-making organizations that use the word "foundation" in their titles should be included in this category. The National Science Foundation and the Empire State Foundation, for example, are not private tax-exempt entities and, therefore, their grants should not be included in a report of private voluntary support.
    f. **Corporations:** Corporations, partnerships, and cooperatives that have been organized for profit-making purposes include corporations owned by individuals and families and other closely held companies. Also included in this category are business-sponsored foundations (i.e., those organizations that have been created by business corporations and have been funded exclusively by their companies). Also included are industry trade associations.
    g. **Religious organizations:** Includes churches, synagogues, and temples and their denominational entities, hierarchies, orders, and service groups.
    h. **Fund-raising consortia:** Entities that have been formed by a group of cooperating institutions or organizations for the purpose of facilitating their fund-raising activities. Examples: The United Negro College fund and the Virginia Council of Independent Colleges are examples of entities to be considered fund-raising consortia other than governmental agencies.
    i. **Other organizations:** All organizations not defined above as foundations, corporations and businesses, religious organizations, or fund-raising consortia other than governmental agencies. Examples include fraternal organizations. Alumni association gifts should be counted as coming from alumni.
    j. **Bequests:** Note that these are bequests actually received during the reporting year.

32. **Government appropriations:**
    a. **Government appropriations (Federal, State & Local):** Revenues received by an institution through acts of a legislative body, except grants and contracts. These funds are for meeting current operating expenses and not for specific projects or programs. Examples are the state's general appropriation and the federal land grant appropriation.
    b. **Government grants and contracts:** Revenues from governmental agencies that are for specific research projects or other types of programs. Examples are research projects, training programs, and similar activities for which amounts are received or expenditures are reimbursable under the terms of a government grant or contract. Includes Pell Grants.

33. **Hospitals (expenditures):** Expenditures associated with the operation of a hospital, including nursing expenses, other professional services, general services, administrative services, fiscal services, and charges for physical plant operations.

. . . .

34. Hospitals (revenues): Include a hospital operated by the institution and clinics associated with training. Include gifts, grants, appropriations, research revenues, and endowment income. Exclude clinics that are part of the student health services program. Include all amounts appropriated by governments for the operation of hospitals. Exclude medical schools.

35. Independent operations (expenditures): Expenditures for operations that are independent of or unrelated to the primary missions of the institution (i.e., instruction, research, public service) although they may contribute indirectly to the enhancement of these programs.

36. Independent operations (revenues): Revenues associated with operations independent of or unrelated to the primary missions of the institution (i.e., instruction, research, public service) although they may contribute indirectly to the enhancement of these programs. This category generally includes only those revenues associated with major federally funded research and development centers.

37. In-state student: A student who is a legal resident of the state in which the institution is located.

38. Institutional loans (number of students with): Students who pay for all or part of their educational expenses with funds that have been loaned by the institution.

39. Institutional scholarships and fellowships (expenditures): That portion of total expenditures for scholarships and fellowships that is financed by the institution. (See "scholarships and fellowships.")

40. Institutional support (expenditures): Expenditures for the day-to-day operational support of the institution. Includes expenditures for general administrative services, executive direction and planning, legal and fiscal operations, and public relations and development. Excludes expenditures for physical plant operations.

41. Instruction (expenditures): Expenditures of the colleges, schools, departments, and other instructional divisions of the institution and expenditures for departmental research and public service that are not separately budgeted. Includes expenditures for credit and non-credit activities. Excludes expenditures for academic administration where the primary function is administration (e.g., academic deans). Also includes general academic instruction, occupational and vocational instruction, special session instruction, community education, preparatory and adult basic education, and remedial and tutorial instruction conducted by the teaching faculty for the institution's students.

42. IPEDS (Integrated Postsecondary Education Data System) survey form names:
   a.   IPEDS EF-1 and IPEDS EF-2: Fall Enrollment Survey
   b.   IPEDS F-1 and F-1A: Finance Survey
   c.   IPEDS L: Academic Libraries Survey

43. Libraries (expenditures): The funds expended from the library budget regardless of when the funds may have been received from federal, state, or other sources. Includes salaries and wages, print materials, current serial subscriptions, microforms, machine-readable materials, audiovisual materials, other collection expenditures, preservation, furniture and equipment, computer hardware, postage, telecommunications, on-line database searches, contracted computer services, and all other operating expenditures. Excludes salaries and wages for maintenance and custodial staff, microcomputer software used only by library staff, and expenditures for capital outlays. Also, expenditures for all print material, microfilm, microfiche, audiovisual materials such as records and films, and computer software. Excludes expenditures for hardware of any kind (e.g., computer terminals, microfiche readers, record players, and projectors).

44. Long-term debt: Includes bonds and other forms of long-term debt used to finance construction or renovation of buildings or other capital projects, as well as the refinancing of previous bond issues that have become due; funds normally recorded in the financial statements under "net investment in plant" used for the acquisition of land and buildings; short-term obligations excluded from current liabilities; amounts of assets or future revenue streams pledged to outstanding debt.

45. Mandatory transfers: Transfers from current funds to other funds that must be made in order to fulfill a binding legal obligation of the institution. Includes amounts for debt repayment, required provisions for plant renewals and replacements, and grant agreements with government agencies, donors, and other organizations to match gifts and grants to loan and other funds.

46. Market value (fair value) of endowment: Quoted market prices of monetary and non-monetary endowment assets. If quoted market prices are not available, fair value may be estimated based on quoted market prices for similar assets, independent appraisals, or valuation techniques, such as the present value of estimated future cash flows.

47. **Market value (fair value) of new planned gifts:** The present value of estimated future cash flows from new planned gifts using a discount rate commensurate with the risks involved.
48. **Net realizable value of new planned gifts:** Market (or fair) value minus an estimate of uncollectible gifts.
49. **Non-tenured faculty:** Faculty on a track to be considered for permanence of position, as yet undecided.
50. **Non-tenure-line faculty:** A faculty position, or a person occupying a faculty position, which is not eligible for tenure. Includes all faculty in institutions that do not award tenure.
51. **Other revenue sources:** Revenues not covered elsewhere. Examples are interest income and gains (net of losses) from investments of unrestricted current funds, miscellaneous rentals and sales, expired term endowments, and terminated annuity or life income agreements, if not material. Also includes revenues resulting from the sales and services of internal service departments to persons or agencies external to the institution (e.g., the sale of computer time).
52. **Part-time students:**
    a. **Undergraduate**: A student enrolled for either 11 semester credits or less, or 11 quarter credits or less, or less than 24 contact hours a week each term; a student enrolled in a 4-year or 5-year bachelor's degree program, in an associate's degree program, or in a vocational or technical program below the baccalaureate for either 11 semester credits or less; or 11 quarter credits or less; or less than 24 contact hours a week each term;
    b. **Graduate:** A student enrolled for either 8 semester credits or less, or 8 quarter credits or less.
53. **Plant depreciation identified during the year:** Book or replacement value of plant assets recognized as "used up" or depleted during the year.
54. **Plant operations and maintenance (expenditures):** Expenditures for operations established to provide service and maintenance related to campus grounds and facilities used for educational and general purposes.
55. **Private gifts, grants, contracts (revenues):** Revenues from private donors for which no legal consideration is involved and from private contracts for specific goods and services provided to the funding agent as stipulation for receipt of the funds. Includes only those gifts grants, and contracts that are directly related to instruction, research, public service, or other institutional purposes. Includes monies received as a result of gifts, grants, or contracts from a foreign government. Also includes the estimated dollar amount of contributed services.
56. **Public Service (expenditures):** Funds budgeted specifically for public service and expended for activities established primarily to provide non-instructional services beneficial to groups external to the institution. Examples are seminars and projects provided to particular sectors of the community and expenditures for community services and cooperative extension services.
57. **Pure (or true) endowment:** Funds whose principal is non-expendable and that are intended to be invested to provide earning for institutional use; endowment assets are donated by individuals or organizations to provide permanent capital and an ongoing stream of current income for an institution. Excludes life income and annuity funds.
58. **Quasi-endowment:** Funds established by the governing board to function like an endowment fund but which may be totally expended at any time at the discretion of the governing board.
59. **Replacement value of new investment in plant:** The cost to replace all buildings acquired during the year. (See **6. Beginning-of-year replacement value of plant** for details.)
60. **Sales and services of affiliated hospitals:** Revenues generated by a hospital operated by the postsecondary institution. Includes gifts, grants, appropriations, research revenues, endowment income, and revenues of health clinics that are part of the hospital unless such clinics are part of the student health services program. Also includes all amounts appropriated by governments (federal, state, local) for the operation of hospitals.
61. **Sales and services of auxiliary enterprises:** Revenues generated by or collected from the auxiliary enterprise operations of the institution that exist to furnish a service to students, faculty, or staff, and that charge a fee that is directly related to, although not necessarily equal to, the cost of the service. Auxiliary enterprises are managed as essentially self-supporting activities. Examples are residence halls, food services, student health services, college stores, and movie theaters.
62. **Sales and services of educational activities:** Revenues from the sales of goods or services that are incidental to the conduct of instruction, research or public service. Examples include film rentals, sales of scientific and literary publications, testing services, university presses, dairy products, machine shop products, data processing services, cosmetology services, and sales of handcrafts prepared in classes.

63. Scholarships and fellowships (expenditures): Expenditures made in the form of outright grants-in-aid, tuition and fee waivers, prizes, and trainee stipends to individuals enrolled in formal undergraduate or graduate course work, either for credit or non-credit. Includes Pell Grants, aid from other Federal, state and local government agencies, private sources, and aid to students in the form of tuition or fee remissions. Excludes those remissions that are granted because of faculty or staff status, or for which services to the institution must be rendered, such as payment for teaching, or student loans. Also excludes College Work-Study Program expenses.

64. Short-term debt: Debt that normally is to be repaid in full over a period of a year or less.

65. Sources of funds expended for sponsored research (see **66. Sponsored research [expenditures]** for definition of "sponsored research")::
   a. U.S. government: Units or agencies of the Federal government.
   b. State and local government: Units or agencies of state, county, city, or other local governments.
   c. U.S. corporations: Corporations headquartered in the U.S. ("Corporation" is defined in **31 f. Corporations**).
   d. Private U.S. foundations: See **31 e. Private foundations**.
   e. Bequests and gifts from living individuals: Bequests actually received and other support from individuals.
   f. Foreign governments, private foundations, and corporations: Units or agencies of non-U.S. governments, private foreign foundations (see **31 e. Private foundations**), and foreign corporations (see **31 f. Corporations**).
   g. Other outside sponsors: Any external source not accounted for in the above categories.
   h. Institutional funds: Funds separately budgeted by an organizational unit within the institution.

66. Sponsored research (expenditures): Funds expended for activities specifically organized to produce research outcomes and commissioned by an agency either external to the institution or separately budgeted by an organizational unit within the institution.

67. Students by race/ethnicity: Categories used to describe groups to which individuals belong, identify with, or belong in the eyes of the community. The categories do not denote scientific definitions of anthropological origins. A person may be counted in only one group. The groups used to categorize U.S. citizens and resident aliens (holders of Form I-551/155) are: Black, non-Hispanic; Native American; Asian or Pacific Islander; Hispanic; and White, non-Hispanic, defined as follows:
   a. Black, non-Hispanic: A person having origins in any of the black racial groups of Africa, except those of Hispanic origin.
   b. Native American: A person having origins in any of the original peoples of North America and who maintains cultural identification through tribal affiliation or community recognition, including those groups considered American Indians or Alaskan Natives.
   c. Asian or Pacific Islander: A person having origins in any of the original peoples of the Far East, Southeast Asia, the Indian Subcontinent, or Pacific Islands. This includes people from China, Japan, Korea, the Philippine Islands, American Samoa, India, and Vietnam.
   d. Hispanic: A person of Mexican, Puerto Rican, Cuban, Central or South American or other Latino culture or origin, regardless of race.
   e. White, non-Hispanic: A person having origins in any of the original peoples of Europe, North Africa, or the Middle East (except those of Hispanic origin).

68. Student services (expenditures): Funds expended for admissions, registrar activities, and activities whose primary purpose is to contribute to students' emotional and physical well-being and to their intellectual, cultural, and social development outside the context of the formal instructional program. Examples are career guidance, counseling, financial aid administration, and student health services (except when operated as a self-supporting auxiliary enterprise).

69. Students from outside the U.S. and Canada: Students who are not legal residents of the U.S. or Canada.

70. Tenured faculty: Persons occupying a faculty position with permanent status.

71. Term endowment: Funds for which the donor has stipulated that the principal may be expended after a stated period or on the occurrence of a certain event.

72. **Total assets:** The accumulated total for all fund groups of assets such as cash, receivables, amounts due from other fund groups, investments, securities, undrawn appropriations, inventories, prepaid expenses, deferred charges, land, buildings, improvements, equipment, and books.

73. **Total credit hours produced by selected departments/divisions:** Total number of credit hours taught by faculty in a particular department or division. A credit hour is a unit of measure representing an hour (50 minutes) of instruction over a 15-week period in a semester or trimester system or a 10-week period in a quarter system. It is applied toward the total number of hours needed to complete the requirements for a degree, diploma, certificate, or other formal award.

74. **Total employees:** All individuals paid directly or indirectly by the institution, including those classified as executive, administrative, and managerial; faculty; teaching and research assistants; other professionals; technical and paraprofessionals; clerical and secretarial; skilled crafts; and service/maintenance. Exclude casual employees and students in the College Work-Study Program.

75. **Total liabilities:** The accumulated total for all fund groups of obligations such as accounts and notes payable, accrued liabilities, indebtedness, and amounts due to other fund groups.

76. **Total return on endowment:** Endowment yield plus appreciation (or depreciation) of endowment assets.

77. **Transfer undergraduate applicants:** Applicants for admission to the institution known to have previously attended a postsecondary institution at the undergraduate level. These students may transfer with or without credit. Excludes students applying for the fall term who attend college for the first time in the prior summer term; also excludes students admitted for advanced standing (college credits earned before graduation from high school).

78. **Transfer undergraduate applicants accepted:** Transfer applicants accepted for admission for the first time at the undergraduate level.

79. **Transfer undergraduate applicants who matriculated:** Entering undergraduate transfer students who are enrolled full-time (see "full-time students") or entering graduate transfer students who are enrolled full time or part time (see "full-time students" and "part-time students").

80. **Unexpended plant funds balance:** Unexpended resources derived from various sources to finance the acquisition of long-lived plant assets and the associated liabilities.

Calculation of Indicators

Indicators and other statistics included in this book were derived or calculated as follows:

FINANCIAL CAPITAL

Revenues

Note: Total current fund revenues = tuition and fee income + federal appropriations + state appropri + local appropriations + federal grants and contracts + state grants and contracts + local grants and contracts + private gifts, grants, and contracts + endowment support for operations + sales and servic educational activities + sales and services of auxiliary enterprises + sales and services of hospitals + sources + independent operations.

Tuition and fees as a percent of total current fund revenues: tuition and fee income ÷ total curre fund revenues. Page 5.

State appropriations as a percent of total current fund revenues: state appropriations ÷ total cur fund revenues. Page 7.

Local appropriations as a percent of total current fund revenues: local appropriations ÷ total cu fund revenues. Page 7.

Federal grants and contracts as a percent of total current fund revenues: federal grants and contracts ÷ total current fund revenues. Page 10.

Private gifts, grants, and contracts as a percent of total current fund revenues: private gifts, gr and contracts ÷ total current fund revenue. Page 12.

Endowment support for operations as a percent of total current fund revenues: endowment sup for operations ÷ total current fund revenues. Page 14.

Sales and services of auxiliary enterprises as a percent of total current fund revenues: sales an services of auxiliary enterprises ÷ total current fund revenues. Page 16.

Sources of revenue for sponsored research: total revenues for sponsored research = total U.S. government funds + total state and local government funds + U.S. corporate funds + private U.S. foundation funds + bequests and gifts from living individuals + funds from foreign governments, pri foundations, and corporations + funds from other outside sources + institutional funds. Page 19.

Expenditures

Note: Total current fund expenditures (including mandatory transfers) = expenditures for instructio sponsored research + public service + academic support + student services + institutional support + p operations and maintenance + auxiliary enterprises + hospitals + independent operations + scholarsh and fellowships.

Instructional expenditures as a percent of total current fund expenditures: instructional expenditures ÷ total current fund expenditures + mandatory transfers. Page 24.

Academic support expenditures as a percent of total current fund expenditures: academic support expenditures ÷ total current fund expenditures + mandatory transfers. Page 28.

Plant operations and maintenance expenditures as a percent of total current fund expenditures: plant operations and maintenance expenditures ÷ total current fund expenditures + mandatory transfers. Page 76.

Instructional expenditures per FTE student: instructional expenditures ÷ FTE students. Note: FTE students = all full-time headcount students + (part-time headcount students ÷ 3). Page 24.

<u>Assets, liabilities, funds balances</u>

Excess (deficit) of current fund revenues over current fund expenditures: current fund revenues ÷ (current fund expenditures + mandatory transfers). Page 30.

Current fund balance 1994-95 as a percent of current fund balance 1993-94: current fund balance 1994-95 ÷ current fund balance 1993-94. Page 30.

Long-term debt as a percent of total liabilities: long-term debt ÷ total liabilities. Page 35.

Total assets as a percent of total liabilities: total assets ÷ total liabilities. Page 37.

Market value of endowment as a percent of total assets: end-of-year market value of endowment [book value of pure + term + quasi] ÷ total assets. Page 39.

Market value of endowment per FTE student: end-of-year market value of endowment ÷ FTE students. Page 39.

Yield as a percent of total endowment: endowment yield ÷ end-of-year market value of endowment. Page 42.

Total return on endowment as a percent of total endowment: total return on endowment ÷ end-of-year market value of endowment. Page 42.

End-of-year market value of total endowment as a percent of beginning-of-year value: end-of-year market value of total endowment ÷ beginning-of-year market value of endowment. Page 42.

Quasi endowment as a percent of total endowment: quasi endowment ÷ end-of-year market value of endowment. Page 48.

Fund-Raising

Note: Total gifts = gifts from alumni + gifts from parents + gifts from other individuals +gifts from private foundations + gifts from corporations + gifts from religious organizations + gifts from fund-raising consortia + gifts from other organizations + bequests received. (Does not include planned gifts.)

Gifts from alumni as a percent of total gifts: gifts from alumni ÷ total gifts. Page 53.

Gifts from parents as a percent of total gifts: gifts from parents ÷ total gifts. Page 53.

Gifts from other individuals as a percent of total gifts: gifts from other individuals ÷ total gifts. Page 53.

Gifts from trustees (including public university foundation trustees) as a percent of total gifts: gifts from trustees ÷ total gifts. Page 53.

Gifts from private foundations as a percent of total gifts: gifts from private foundations ÷ total gifts. Page 59.

Gifts from corporations as a percent of total gifts: gifts from corporations ÷ total gifts. Page 59.

Gifts from religious organizations as a percent of total gifts: gifts from religious organizations ÷ total gifts. Page 59.

Gifts from fund-raising consortia as a percent of total gifts: gifts from fund-raising consortia ÷ total gifts. Page 59.

Gifts from other organizations as a percent of total gifts: gifts from other organizations ÷ total gifts. Page 59.

Bequests received as a percent of total gifts: bequests received ÷ total gifts. Page 66.

Market value of new planned gifts as a percent of total gifts actually received: market value of new planned gifts ÷ total gifts. Page 66.

Net realizable value of new planned gifts as a percent of total gifts actually received: net realizable value of new planned gifts ÷ total gifts. Page 66.

Percent of living alumni who have given at any time in the past 5 years: total living alumni who have given any time during the past five years ÷ total living alumni. Page 72.

PHYSICAL CAPITAL

End-of-year replacement value of plant as a percent of beginning-of-year replacement value of plant: end-of-year replacement value of plant ÷ beginning-of-year replacement value of plant. Page 78.

198   **Calculation of Indicators**

· ·

Estimated maintenance backlog of total plant as a percent of total replacement value of plant: estimated maintenance backlog of total plant ÷ end-of-year replacement value of plant. Page 81.

New investment in plant as a percent of plant depreciation at replacement value: replacement value of new investment in plant ÷ plant depreciation at replacement value. Page 83.

New investment in plant as a percent of plant depreciation at book value: replacement value of new investment in plant ÷ plant depreciation at book value. Page 83.

INFORMATION CAPITAL

Book and monograph volumes per FTE student: total book and monograph volumes ÷ FTE students. Page 88.

Percent of institutions with a "chief information officer:" total institutions with a chief information officer ÷ total institutions responding to the question. Page 101.

Percent of institutions with a formal policy for funding depreciation of computer equipment: total institutions with a formal policy for funding depreciation of computer equipment ÷ total institutions responding to the question. Page 97.

Percent of institutions with a campus-wide network: total institutions with a campus-wide network ÷ total institutions responding to the question. Page 94.

Percent of networks with fiber optic central spine: total institutions with fiber optic central spine ÷ total institutions with a campus-wide network. Page 94.

Percent of networks with coaxial cable central spine: total institutions with coaxial cable central spine ÷ total institutions with a campus-wide network. Page 94.

Percent of networks with other central spine: total institutions with a central spine other than fiber optic or coaxial cable ÷ total institutions with a campus-wide network. Page 94.

Percent of institutions with library catalog on the network: total institutions with library catalog on the network ÷ total institutions with a campus-wide network. Page 94.

Percent of administrative offices with connections to the network: total institutions with connections to the network ÷ total institutions with a campus-wide network. Page 94.

Percent of faculty/staff offices with connections to the network: total faculty/staff offices with connections to the network ÷ total institutions with a campus-wide network. Page 94.

Percent of libraries with connections to the network: total libraries with connections to the network ÷ total institutions with a campus-wide network. Page 94.

Percent of classrooms/labs with connections to the network: total classrooms/labs with connections to the network ÷ total institutions with a campus-wide network. Page 94.

Percent of student rooms with connections to the network: total student rooms with connections to the network ÷ total institutions with a campus-wide network. Page 94.

Percent of institutions with networks that provide full Internet access: total institutions with full Internet access ÷ total institutions with a campus-wide network. Page 90.

Percent of institutions with networks that provide partial Internet access: total institutions with networks that provide partial Internet access ÷ total institutions with a campus-wide network. Page 90.

Percent of institutions with networks that provide no Internet access: total institutions with networks that provide no Internet access ÷ total institutions with a campus-wide network. Page 90.

Percent of institutions with Internet connections that provide access to E-mail: total institutions with Internet connections that provide access to E-mail ÷ total institutions with full or partial access to the Internet. Page 90.

Percent of institutions with Internet connections that provide access to Gopher: total institutions with Internet connections that provide access to Gopher ÷ total institutions with full or partial access to the Internet. Page 90.

Percent of institutions with Internet connections that provide access to FTP: total institutions with Internet connections that provide access to FTP ÷ total institutions with full or partial access to the Internet. Page 90.

Percent of institutions with Internet connections that provide access to Telnet: total institutions with Internet connections that provide access to Telnet ÷ total institutions with full or partial access to the Internet. Page 90.

Percent of institutions with Internet connections that provide access to News Lists: total institutions with Internet connections that provide access to News Lists ÷ total institutions with full or partial access to the Internet. Page 90.

Percent of institutions with Internet connections that provide access to List Serves: total institutions with Internet connections that provide access to List Serves ÷ total institutions with full or partial access to the Internet. Page 90.

FTE students per personal computer or terminal supplied for student use: FTE students ÷ total number of personal computers and/or terminals supplied for student use. Page 97.

Percent of institutions that require full-time undergraduates to have computers: total institutions that require full-time undergraduates to have computers ÷ total institutions responding to the question. Page 97.

Percent of institutions that require part-time undergraduates to have computers: total institutions that require part-time undergraduates to have computers ÷ total institutions responding to the question. Page 97.

HUMAN CAPITAL

Note: full-time equivalent students or faculty members = the sum of all full-time headcount students or faculty members, plus one-third of all part-time headcount students or faculty members.

Students—Enrollment

Percent of total FTE students who are part-time: total FTE students who are part-time ÷ total FTE students. Page 107.

Fall 1994 total FTE students as a percent of fall 1993 total FTE students: fall 1994 total FTE students ÷ fall 1993 total FTE students. Page 104.

Black FTE students as a percent of total FTE students: Black FTE students ÷ total FTE students. Page 110.

Asian FTE students as a percent of total FTE students: Asian FTE students ÷ total FTE students. Page 110.

Hispanic FTE students as a percent of total FTE students: Hispanic FTE students ÷ total FTE students. Page 110.

Female FTE students as a percent of total FTE students: female FTE students ÷ total FTE students. Page 113.

Students—Admissions

Percent of freshman applicants accepted: total freshman applicants accepted ÷ total completed freshman applications. Page 121.

Percent of accepted freshman who matriculate: total accepted freshman applicants who matriculate ÷ total freshman applicants accepted. Page 124.

Percent of transfer applicants accepted: total transfer applicants accepted ÷ total completed transfer applications. Page 121.

Percent of accepted transfers who matriculate: total accepted transfer applicants who matriculate ÷ total transfer applicants accepted. Page 124.

Percent of total students from within the state: total students from within the state ÷ total students. Page 119.

Percent of total students from outside the U.S. And Canada: total students from outside the U.S. And Canada ÷ total students. Page 119.

Associate degrees awarded as a percent of FTE enrollment: associate degrees awarded ÷ FTE students. Page 127.

Baccalaureate degrees awarded as a percent of FTE enrollment: baccalaureate degrees awarded ÷ FTE students. Page 127.

Master's degrees awarded as a percent of FTE enrollment: master's degrees awarded ÷ FTE students. Page 127.

<u>**Students—Tuition, Fees, and Financial Aid**</u>

Institutional scholarships and fellowships as a percent of total tuition and fee income: institutional scholarships and fellowships ÷ tuition and fee income. Page 132.

Tuition and fees per undergraduate student (private): published tuition and fee charges for private institutions per undergraduate student. Page 136.

Tuition and fees per in-state undergraduate student (public): published tuition and fee charges per in-state undergraduate student. Page 138.

Tuition and fees per undergraduate out-of-state student (public): published tuition and fee charges per out-of-state undergraduate student. Page 138.

Percent of students with institutional scholarships and fellowships: students with institutional scholarships and fellowships ÷ total students. Page 141.

Percent of students with institutional loans: students with institutional loans ÷ total students. Page 143.

Percent of students with college work-study jobs: students with college work-study jobs ÷ total students. Page 145.

<u>**Faculty**</u>

Note: full-time equivalent faculty members = the sum of all full-time headcount faculty members, plus one-third of all part-time headcount faculty members.

Percent of FTE faculty who are non-tenured: non-tenured FTE faculty ÷ FTE faculty. Page 147.

Percent of FTE faculty who are tenured: tenured FTE faculty ÷ FTE faculty. Page 147.

Percent of FTE faculty who are non-tenure-line: non-tenure-line FTE faculty ÷ FTE faculty. Page 147.

Percent of FTE faculty who are part-time: part-time FTE faculty ÷ FTE faculty. Page 151.

Ratio of FTE business administration majors to FTE business administration faculty: FTE business administration majors ÷ FTE business administration faculty. Page 164.

Ratio of FTE humanities majors to FTE humanities faculty: FTE humanities majors ÷ FTE humanities faculty. Page 164.

Ratio of FTE science/math majors to FTE science/math faculty: FTE science/math majors ÷ FTE science/math faculty. Page 164.

Ratio of FTE social science majors to FTE social science faculty: FTE social science majors ÷ FTE social science faculty. Page 164.

Ratio of FTE health professions majors to FTE health professions faculty: FTE health professions majors ÷ FTE health professions faculty. Page 164.

Ratio of FTE engineering majors to FTE engineering faculty: FTE engineering majors ÷ FTE engineering faculty. Page 164.

Ratio of FTE education majors to FTE education faculty: FTE education majors ÷ FTE education faculty. Page 164.

Business administration department/division credit hour production per FTE faculty member: total business administration department/division credit hour production ÷ FTE business administration faculty. Page 166.

Humanities department/division credit hour production per FTE faculty member: total humanities department/division credit hour production ÷ FTE humanities faculty. Page 166.

Science/math department/division credit hour production per FTE faculty member: total science/math department/division credit hour production ÷ FTE science/math faculty. Page 166.

Social science department/division credit hour production per FTE faculty member: total social science department/division credit hour production ÷ FTE social science faculty. Page 166.

Health professions department/division credit hour production per FTE faculty member: total health professions department/division credit hour production ÷ FTE health professions faculty. Page 166.

Engineering department/division credit hour production per FTE faculty member: total engineering department/division credit hour production ÷ FTE engineering faculty. Page 166.

Education department/division credit hour production per FTE faculty member: total education department/division credit hour production ÷ FTE education faculty. Page 166.

Percent of FTE faculty who are Black: FTE Black faculty ÷ FTE faculty. Page 157.

Percent of FTE faculty who are Asian or Pacific Islander: FTE Asian or Pacific Islander faculty ÷ FTE faculty. Page 157.

Percent of FTE faculty who are Hispanic: FTE Hispanic faculty ÷ FTE faculty. Page 157.

Percent of FTE female faculty who are tenured: FTE tenured female faculty ÷ FTE female faculty. Page 153.

Percent of FTE female faculty who are non-tenure-line: FTE non-tenure-line female faculty ÷ FTE female faculty. Page 153.

Percent of FTE female faculty who are non-tenured: FTE non-tenured female faculty ÷ FTE female faculty. Page 153.

Percent of FTE faculty who are women: FTE female faculty ÷ FTE faculty. Page 153.

Percent of FTE faculty who are over 60: FTE faculty over 60 ÷ FTE faculty. Page 160.

<u>Employment</u>

Faculty headcount fall, 1994 as a percent of faculty headcount fall, 1993: fall 1994 faculty headcount ÷ fall 1993 faculty headcount. Page 168.

FTE faculty fall, 1994 as a percent of FTE faculty fall, 1993: fall 1994 FTE faculty ÷ fall 1993 FTE faculty. Page 168.

Percent of total FTE employees who are faculty: FTE faculty ÷ total FTE employees. Page 171.

Percent of total FTE employees who are executive, administrative, and managerial staff: FTE executive, administrative, and managerial staff ÷ total FTE employees. Page 174.

About the Authors

Barbara E. Taylor was Vice President for Programs and Research at the Association of Governing Boards of Universities and Colleges during the writing of this book. She is currently Senior Associate at the Academic Search Consultation Service in Washington, D.C. Taylor is the author or coauthor of several books, including *The Effective Board of Trustees, Working Effectively With Trustees, Good Stewardship: A Handbook for Seminary Trustees, Strategic Analysis: Using Comparative Data to Understand Your Institution,* and the forthcoming *Improving the Performance of Governing Boards* (Oryx Press, 1996), as well as numerous articles, book chapters, and case studies. She is a trustee of Wittenberg University and a Senior Fellow of the Cheswick Center.

William F. Massy is Professor of Education and Business Administration at Stanford University. After serving in faculty and administrative positions at the Massachusetts Institute of Technology, Massy became a professor and Vice Provost for Research at Stanford, where he later was appointed Vice President for Business and Finance. He founded the Stanford Institute for Higher Education Research in 1989 and served as its director until early 1996. He is the author of numerous books and articles on business administration and higher education, including, most recently, *Resource Allocation in Higher Education* (University of Michigan Press, 1996). He currently directs the Project on Educational Quality of the National Center for Postsecondary Improvement.